Professionalizing
Early Childhood Education
As a Field of Practice

"As Stacie Goffin points out, this is a defining moment for early childhood education. Public need and demand for high-quality early childhood programs continue to grow. Federal and state policies play an important role in early childhood education, but that role should be supportive, not directive or field defining. This will happen only with a unified voice from the early childhood field that articulates how best to prepare, support, compensate, and hold accountable educators and programs for meeting the needs of the children and families they serve. Goffin has put forth a compelling case and framework for moving forward. The field should embrace it and begin the work to 'change from inside out' and become a true profession."

—LAURA BORNFREUND, DEPUTY DIRECTOR, EARLY EDUCATION INITIATIVE
    AT NEW AMERICA

"Stacie Goffin makes a strong case to confront the hard questions that divide the early childhood field of practice. She's right. The time has come to unify and professionalize the field—not just rhetorically but as evidenced by the caliber of interactions with children and their families. We all need to reflect on our roles and rethink our positions if together we are going to reengineer an early care and education system that offers infants, toddlers, and young children the early learning experiences they so richly need and deserve."

—MATTHEW E. MELMED, EXECUTIVE DIRECTOR, ZERO TO THREE

"Few can any longer deny that ECE's fragmentation is hurtful to children and to ECE as a field of practice. Few can now deny that inclusive early learning settings for young children are beneficial to all involved—whether children with typical trajectories of development or those whose development pathways diverge from this trajectory. Fulfilling the aspirations of ECE, though, requires that we enter into the conversations Goffin proposes. Kudos to her for preparing this guide for our journey."

—PAMELA WINTON, PhD, SENIOR SCIENTIST AND DIRECTOR OF OUTREACH,
    FRANK PORTER GRAHAM CHILD DEVELOPMENT INSTITUTE,
    UNIVERSITY OF NORTH CAROLINA–CHAPEL HILL

"For over a decade Stacie Goffin has persuasively argued that leadership is needed within the field to transform it into a coherent, competent, and accountable profession. In this guidebook she defines the hard questions and provides the tools for structuring conversations that will make that vision a reality."

—Paula Jorde Bloom, PhD, Distinguished Professor of Research and Practice, Founder, McCormick Center for Early Childhood Leadership, National Louis University

"Goffin's book provocatively and insightfully sets the stage for 'conversations with intent' about what should define and unite early childhood education as a field of practice. The inclusion of early intervention and early childhood special education in these conversations is critical to ensure all children and each child as well as their families benefit from a competent and unified workforce. The conversations will not be easy, and the questions to be addressed are challenging. The guide-book Goffin has artfully crafted will help stimulate the forms of conversation as well as the collective actions needed to propel us from our present state to a new era—and a unified field of practice."

—Patricia Snyder, PhD, Professor and David Lawrence Jr Endowed Chair in Early Childhood Studies, University of Florida

"In this book, Goffin taps the essence of leadership—the unwillingness to live with the status quo. She continues to compel us to face the reality of the ECE profession. She helps us accept that there are no sidelines in this work so not to bother looking for those seats. We must be 'all in' and thoughtfully engaged in 'conversations with intent' if our intention to professionalize ECE is to become a reality. Her strategies and recommended practices give us the courage to begin the journey, the tools to look inward to identify the challenges, and the belief that, if we embrace our fear and the uncertainty in this work, we can make this happen. We must be brave enough to leave the shore and trust the journey. Only we can make the journey, but the children are worth it."

—Margaret Kreischer, Early Childhood Education Program Consultant, Child Care Concepts and Past Chair of the NAEYC Affiliate Council

"'If the world were ideal, what conditions would need to be in place to structure ECE as a profession?' This question crystalized for me the essence of *Professionalizing Early Childhood Education As a Field of Practice*. We all know the world is not ideal, but we can and should have the courage to improve it with this book by Stacie Goffin. She leads us to think deeply and to take responsibility for the quality of education for young children. The book's practical suggestions for organizing 'conversations with intent' give us exactly the guidance needed to move forward and establish ECE as a field of practice. I am optimistic that we will achieve the goal. Read the book, reflect, invite early educators in your area, follow Goffin's model, facilitate a group, stay connected, and together we will make it happen."

—ANGÈLE SANCHO PASSE, AUTHOR OF *EVALUATING AND SUPPORTING EARLY CHILDHOOD TEACHERS* AND OTHER TITLES, PAST MEMBER OF THE NAEYC GOVERNING BOARD

"In this small but power-packed volume, veteran early childhood educator and child advocate Stacie Goffin takes on the ambiguous and challenging dilemmas of defining ECE as a profession. The book provides a timely call to action for all of us who recognize how typical care and education all too often 'are contrary to our beliefs and knowledge about how best to support children's learning and development.' It is truly a must read for all who care about children!"

—CAROL GARHART MOONEY, EARLY CHILDHOOD EDUCATOR AND AUTHOR, *THEORIES OF PRACTICE: RAISING THE STANDARDS OF EARLY CHILDHOOD EDUCATION*

Professionalizing Early Childhood Education As a Field of Practice

A Guide to the Next Era

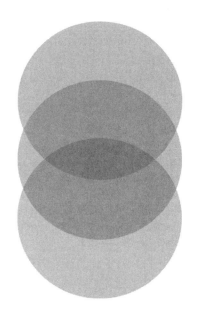

STACIE G. GOFFIN

Redleaf Press®
www.redleafpress.org
800-423-8309

Published by Redleaf Press
10 Yorkton Court
St. Paul, MN 55117
www.redleafpress.org

National Association for the
Education of Young Children
1313 L Street NW, Suite 500
Washington, DC 20005-4101
www.naeyc.org

First edition 2015
Cover and interior design by Jim Handrigan
Typeset in Weiss
Printed in the United States of America
22 21 20 19 18 17 16 15   1 2 3 4 5 6 7 8

Library of Congress Cataloging-in-Publication Data
Goffin, Stacie G.
   Professionalizing early childhood education as a field of practice : a guide to the next era / Stacie G. Goffin.
       pages cm
   Summary: "Professionalizing Early Childhood Education As a Field of Practice is a tool to help everyone in early childhood education engage in serious discussions about professionalizing the field. Author and thought-leader Stacie G. Goffin has written a book that contains an overview of the topic, a participant guide, a conversation workbook, and a facilitator guide; each section supports deep thought and creative discussions about how early childhood education can move toward being a professional field of practice"—Provided by publisher.
   Includes bibliographical references.
   ISBN 978-1-60554-434-2 (paperback)
   1. Early childhood teachers—Training of. 2. Early childhood teachers—Professional ethics. 3. Early childhood education—Study and teaching.   I. Title.
CURR LB1732.3.G64 2015
       372.210973—dc23
                                                                    2015010358

Printed on acid-free paper

NAEYC Item #7232

To those willing to risk the present as we know it to create

a better future for young children and early childhood education

as a field of practice

Contents

Foreword

Sophistication. That is the word that comes to mind when I think about all that needs to happen in order for young children to be prepared for school and life. Whether it is scaffolding language or balancing early learning standards and developmentally appropriate practice, using outdoor play to teach science concepts or charting kindergartners' color preferences to help them understand mathematics applications, these are all examples of what takes place in high-quality early learning environments. At the heart of these environments are early childhood educators—teachers, administrators, paraprofessionals, and family child care home providers. While each of them may have taken a different path to arrive in the early education field, one thing is the same—children, families, communities, and the country are counting on them to deliver on the promise of high-quality early learning.

We have made significant progress in understanding what early childhood educators should know and be able to do. We now have a sharper focus on professional preparation systems (including higher education), and increased public financial investments are being made in early learning. Despite all of this, the field has not yet demanded that we take the next step: to create a professional field of practice. In this, Stacie Goffin's latest book, she challenges early childhood educators not to wait for pressure from the outside, but instead to find the courage and intentionality to be creators of their own destiny.

Among other systems-building strategies, Stacie asks us to contemplate our existing mental models, as they are often deeply embedded and might be obstructing our progress. She encourages us to engage in personal reflection and initiate or participate in conversations with the intent to develop a shared understanding and evolved direction. She reminds us that moving this boulder will take both a personal and collective commitment, and that the action required must come from inside the field. She is right.

For far too long we have approached this conversation from a deficit-based model: we have been too timid, too worried about the unintended consequences, too fearful that there would be winners and losers. All the while the expectations and demands directed toward early childhood educators are increasing, and we have not agreed on and aligned the knowledge, competencies, professional preparation systems, and wage and compensation structures that will attract and retain the most highly qualified professionals. The book has great messages that reinforce that we all need to take a deep breath and imagine what could be, not just what is.

The National Association for the Education of Young Children (NAEYC) has a long history of working on behalf of early childhood educators, and recently the Association has redoubled its efforts. In November 2014, with significant stakeholder input, NAEYC completed a yearlong strategic planning process from which several key promises emerged. First, NAEYC's new mission statement includes language that addresses the association's role in serving the profession:

> Mission Statement: NAEYC promotes high-quality early learning for all children, birth through age eight, by connecting practice, policy, and research. We advance a diverse, dynamic early childhood profession and support all who care for, educate, and work on behalf of young children.

Second, one of the five strategic priorities that emerged focuses on early childhood educators:

> The Profession—Goal: The early childhood education profession exemplifies excellence and is recognized as vital and performing a critical role in society.

NAEYC is prepared to exercise leadership and political capital to ensure this strategic priority is accomplished. A number of efforts are under way, including most notably initial market research for a national early childhood recruitment and retention campaign, the compilation of a national directory of higher education early childhood degree programs, and the piloting of professional development system indicators to measure the progress of state professional preparation systems. Additionally, many NAEYC affiliates are poised to play a leadership role in convening the state and local conversations of intent that Stacie so eloquently describes in this book.

NAEYC is but one voice in a dialogue that Stacie urges us to hold in concentric circles of conversation nationwide. She provides a well-defined framework—and there is a seat at the table for everyone who wants to engage. The time has come to align the sophistication required of early childhood educators with the threshold of skills and competencies that define an early childhood field of practice. It is up to each of us to envision and create the professional field of practice that ensures that all young children are prepared to be successful in school and in life.

Rhian Evans Allvin
Executive Director
National Association for the Education of Young Children

Acknowledgments

IN CHAPTER 1, I STATE that this book has the potential to make this a defining moment for early childhood education (ECE) by helping propel the field into its next era. Reaching a moment like this doesn't happen without many people being able to take credit. We are on the cusp of a budding movement to rethink ECE's structure as a field of practice, enabling it to become more capable of fulfilling its promise. So my first expression of gratitude goes to the many colleagues—too many to name and some of whom are anonymous to me—who are stepping forward to make professionalizing ECE as a field of practice a cause. I also want to thank the many people who have listened to my ideas and helped to make them stronger and clearer.

Also stepping forward is the National Association for the Education of Young Children. Someone questioning me about how NAEYC will be involved in this effort follows almost every presentation I've done on this topic. I'm most appreciative to Rhian Evans Allvin for her foreword and to NAEYC for its decision to make *Professionalizing Early Childhood Education As a Field of Practice: A Guide to the Next Era* a membership benefit. I eagerly anticipate the association's leadership in the context of its new strategic priority that seeks to ensure the ECE profession "exemplifies excellence and is recognized as vital and performing a critical role in society."[1]

Kyra Ostendorf is another of those individuals who has stepped forward. Upon first hearing of my interest in creating a conversation guide, she proposed Redleaf Press as its publisher. She not only shepherded the idea through to acceptance, she also was central in placing its publication on a super-fast track so it would quickly be available. Thanks go to David Heath and his staff, especially Heidi Hogg, Laurie Herrmann, Doug Schmitz, and Jim Handrigan for ensuring the target date for publication came to fruition. David not only is the director of Redleaf Press, he also was my editor, and his commitment to my book and its message came through loud and clear.

Deb Flis, whom I so admire as a friend and colleague, provided a very helpful review before the manuscript was sent to Redleaf Press. So did Michael Koetje, who among other things is president of the Washington Association for the Education of Young Children. Even before knowing about this book, he shared intentions to launch a statewide conversation revolving around the issues raised by my previous book, *Early Childhood Education for a New Era: Leading for Our Profession*. That, of course, made him a perfect person to serve as a reviewer. My deep appreciation as well to the book's endorsers: Pam Winton, Paula Jorde Bloom, Laura Bornfreund, Matthew Melmed, Pat Snyder, Angèle Passe, Carol Garhart Mooney, and Gege Kreischer. What a stellar list of colleagues and endorsements! They represent the broad range of "interests"—policy, higher education, program administration, professional development, and children from birth to age eight— whose engagement with these conversations will be crucial to advancing ECE as a professional field of practice.

Because of the tight publication time frame, my husband, Bruce, had to endure my being immersed in the book's development for an intense period of time. As always, he was gracious, accepting, and supportive. Thank you, Bruce, and Dave and Sabra too and, of course, Maya, who brings us so much joy. I know I'm an incredibly lucky person.

CHAPTER 1

Moving Early Childhood Education Forward as a Professional Field of Practice

FEW OF US FAMILIAR with early childhood education (ECE) are unaware of its struggle to fulfill its ambitions as a field of practice.[1] Even though in recent years ECE has experienced significant increases in policy support and funding, the field continues to be characterized by sector fragmentation, reliance on an underdeveloped workforce, and uneven public respect, resulting in a divided field of practice, patchy policy support, and capricious public financing. Further exacerbating the field's status is its historic reluctance to step forward and create a desired future for ECE as a field of practice.

As Jeffrey Conklin has noted, fragmentation represents a phenomenon that pulls apart something that potentially should be whole.[2] Consider the following: Other than working with children or on their behalf, few commonalities bind ECE in terms of shared knowledge, preparation, qualifications, commitments, or aspirations. Rarely do we think of ourselves as part of something larger than our individual programs or separate sectors. As a field, we lack common expectations for the knowledge, skills, dispositions, or preparation teachers need for effective practice. As a result, the cohesion necessary for ensuring ECE's practitioners consistently and competently facilitate children's learning and development is lacking.[3]

Fueled by findings from brain science and evaluations of high-quality ECE programs, immense resources have been directed toward reducing learning gaps between low-income kindergartners and their more advantaged peers. This has resulted in an unprecedented spotlight being aimed at ECE over the past three decades. Yet despite this surge in policy and public interest

- too many children are losing ground, and too many others are not accessing their potential;

- notable gains exist in ECE's knowledge base, but as a field of practice, they're neither widely understood nor applied;

- increased expectations exist for ECE's contributions to children's successful kindergarten entry, but the field lacks the ability to fulfill them;

- the field's increasingly complex systems of delivery, uneven funding, and variable standards undermine a more coherent approach for achieving consistent results across settings; and

- others, impatient with the field's relative passivity, have stepped into the leadership void.[4]

This composite portrayal is discouraging at best. While growing in sophistication as a field of practice, ECE at this point in its evolution can best be described as a field whose occupational configuration—meaning the way in which the field's components are arranged in relation to one another—is unsuited to its current realities.

Having acknowledged its present state, what follows is further explanation for the field's need to step forward to co-create an alternative future for ECE as a field of practice and for the children and families it serves. *Professionalizing Early Childhood Education As a Field of Practice: A Guide to the Next Era*, however, moves beyond my earlier efforts to present the case for rethinking ECE as a field of practice by identifying questions that will need to be addressed and the individual and collective skills that will be required to answer them. This first chapter concludes with an overview of this guide, its purpose, and its organization.

STEPPING FORWARD TO BECOME AN ORGANIZED FIELD OF PRACTICE

This is a defining moment for ECE. Families and leaders in the public, nonprofit, and private sectors are all demanding more of ECE. Yet studies too often document that ECE's practitioners do not foster early learning in ways that fulfill expectations[5]—not only the general public's but also our own as a field. According to a citation by Steven Barnett, between 35 and 45 percent of children entering kindergarten are ill prepared to succeed in school.[6]

During the past half-century of exponential growth, the field has largely reacted to its changing circumstances. Instead of stepping forward in response to new realities and differently envisioning ECE as a field of practice in order to elevate collective competence, the field has looked to others to do the heavy lifting. Most especially, it has relied on advocates, policy makers, and individuals with business and financial clout to expand public recognition of ECE's importance and enlarge public financing.

Spurred by the field's inaction, these supporters have begun defining ECE as a field of practice. While partnering with families, business, and government is essential to achieving the learning and development results wanted for children, the consequences of ECE's external orientation are defining decrees from those outside the field. Unfortunately, these decrees too often are contrary to our beliefs and knowledge about how best to support children's learning and development.

The time has come for the ECE field to step forward and *change from inside out*—to retreat from over-reliance on policy makers and others as change agents on ECE's behalf. Altering the discouraging facts listed earlier depends on our field accepting responsibility for its practitioners' competency and their contributions to children's learning and development. ECE needs to become accountable as a field of practice and be the change agent in defining what this means.

ECE has long claimed the mantle of professionalism, and by almost all indicators the nature of its work aligns with that of a profession. Yet as a field of practice, ECE lacks the attributes associated with recognized professions:

- clarity of shared purpose;

- organizing structures and supportive institutions that bound practitioners by common knowledge and skills;

- clear scopes of practice;

- responsibility for evolving and applying a specialized knowledge base; and

- acceptance of the ethical responsibility to perform consistently at a level of competence capable of promoting children's learning and development.[7]

By structuring ECE as a profession, the field can create a cohesive occupational configuration aligned with its values and beliefs and with the systemic capacity to offer learning and development opportunities associated with children's positive growth.

ORGANIZING AS A PROFESSIONAL FIELD OF PRACTICE

In return for its unique societal contribution, a profession is granted autonomy as a field of practice, but this independence is coupled with certain responsibilities. A profession is expected to continually develop its expert knowledge base, given authority over its use in practice, and held accountable for monitoring members' ethical and competent performance. A profession's mandate is realized through interdependent systems of preparation, practice, and accountability, making professions unique in their occupational structure.

At their core, systems are about the interconnections among their elements.[8] The connections and relationships within and across professions' three primary system components are central to their coherence and effectiveness. By moving beyond its fragmented occupational configuration and structuring itself as a professional field of practice, ECE's potential can be more fully realized.

> **DEFINITIONS**
>
> - A *field* is an invisible world filled with mediums of connections: an invisible structure that connects.[1]
> - The term *field of practice* makes explicit that the purpose of the field in question revolves around performance of a specialized and shared competence.[2]
> - *Professions* are coherent, interconnected systems of preparation, practice, and responsibility.[3]
> - "A *system* is a set of things (people, cells, molecules, or whatever) interconnected in such a way that they produce their own pattern of behavior over time. The system may be buffeted, constricted, triggered, or driven by outside forces. But the system's response to these forces is characteristic of itself, and that response is seldom simple in the real world. In essence, systems cause their own behavior."[4]
> - "*Mental models* are deeply ingrained assumptions, generalizations, or even pictures or images that influence how we understand the world and how we take action."[5]

In 1996 Sharon Kagan and Nancy Cohen presented the first comprehensive vision for an ECE system.[9] Since then, the field has focused on developing its infrastructure and easing the fragmented relationships embedded within and across policy, program delivery, and financing. Systems work related to professional development has attended primarily to cultivating coordination across the field's varied education and training programs, expanding access, and creating career lattices. With growing recognition of teacher-child interactions as central to children's learning and development, the work within this systems domain is also increasingly attending to teachers' instructional and relationship skills.

Absent from these systemic pursuits has been attention to structuring ECE as an *organized field of practice*, one unified by shared purpose and tightly bound by systems of preparation, practice, and accountability. Beyond providing for consistently competent practice, the resultant system would form the nucleus around which delivery, policy, and financing systems should be adjusted, developed, and coordinated.[10] Tying infrastructure development to its formation as a professional field of practice can provide the unifying, systemic, occupational structure needed by ECE to ratchet up the quality, effectiveness, and consistency of its practices across early learning settings.

Rethinking ECE as cohesive systems joined together by common purpose, a specialized knowledge base, required practice standards, and agreed-upon expectations for practitioners represents a paradigm shift. ECE would become a field of practice that accepts responsibility for realizing desired results for children. Among the benefits is establishing the accountability necessary for partnering with policy makers and others to increase field-wide capacity, which will enable the field's societal contributions to become more widely available.

Embracing the merit of structuring ECE as a professional field of practice can redefine the field's trajectory, unleash its potential, and raise its esteem in the public's eyes. Although attending to children's and families' current early learning needs must remain part of our commitment to them in the present, solutions to these problems are inadequate to society's long-term need for a competent field of practice capable of promoting every child's early learning and development. The time has come for envisioning an alternative future for ECE as a field of practice and determining how it will be achieved.

The time has come for envisioning an alternative future for ECE.

This is a daring proposal, one whose fulfillment asks the ECE field to mobilize its collective will to

- take charge of change;

- become a self-governing, clearly delineated field of practice bound by common purpose and destiny; and

- replace its fragmented configuration with an occupational structure responsive to society's need for children who are capable of making the most of their learning potential.

Professions offer a field-unifying strategy designed to bring an occupation's members together around common purpose, collective expertise, and who is served.

They hold their members accountable for competent practices and responsible outcomes. Public esteem is based on an occupation's contribution of its specialized knowledge and skills to society's well-being—knowledge and skills not readily found in society at large. This, in turn, creates the need for formal and specialized preparation and oversight of practice. Finally, professions proactively exercise leadership that facilitates field-wide adaptation to new circumstances, seizes opportunities for improving practice, and advocates for conditions that make competent practice possible and accessible.[11] Not only can this increase children's chances of fulfilling their potential, it can do the same for ECE as a field of practice.

ENGAGING WITH ECE'S CHALLENGE

Organizing ECE as a profession will demand collective resolve to align the field's espoused values and aspirations with the realities of its occupational configuration and uneven expectations for practitioners. Too often, those of us in ECE resist doing what we know to be necessary for achieving good results for children. We tolerate poor performance from colleagues and ourselves and sidestep change, rather than grapple with thorny issues and challenging choices. At the risk of sounding preachy, taking a stand on the caliber and impact of our collective practice is part of our field's moral task.

Learning from Those Who Have Preceded Us

Even though the field's desired future state has been articulated, ECE's configuration as a profession is unknown at present, as are the steps for getting there. The systemic change that lies ahead is best achieved through collective leadership and the real-time learning that comes from immersing in a complex change process that involves

- opening up to multiple perspectives and interpretations of the field's present status within and across its sectors and stakeholders;

- facing difficult truths about current realities;

- letting go of individual and collective thinking once defended as sacrosanct;

- figuring out how to rearrange ECE's systems as a coherent whole instead of focusing on adjusting individual parts;

- fostering generative conversations that spawn new possibilities; and

- joining together to bring a coimagined future to fruition.[12]

This will be a complex undertaking. Yet once united around a vision for the field's future, the shared image of what we're trying to create will focus and channel the purposefulness and energy of our systems change efforts.[13] This means, though, that "one needs to know what the profession aims to do,"[14] and we create "the capacity to hold a shared picture of the future we want to create."[15]

Professionalizing Early Childhood Education As a Field of Practice: A Guide to the Next Era was written to move ECE beyond its longstanding impasse regarding the field's purpose and responsibility. This stalemate has stymied our ability to progress as a field of practice and become "whole." Study of other professions makes evident that the process of professionalizing will involve an extended developmental journey that requires

- identifying ECE's unique contribution to society's well-being;

- ascertaining its specialized expertise;

- forging a shared commitment to fulfilling its purpose; and

- navigating currents of the field's social and economic contexts.[16]

Participants experienced with similar journeys recount that actions and decisions typically emerge while engaged with the work. As Peter Senge and his colleagues have forecast, "Like others before you, you will discover much of the plot as you invent it."[17]

Those of us engaged in systems work can relate to the accuracy of this last statement. This reality may be uncomfortable, though, for those preferring linear planning and clearly identified and timed benchmarks. The literature on systems change, however, makes it clear that ECE's next step begins with

- creating the conditions for seeing and thinking differently, both individually and together;

- accepting that definitive answers don't yet exist; and

- learning from and nurturing the collective intelligence, creativity, and experimentation that emerges over time.

Resolving tough, adaptive challenges requires flexibility. The need to be open-minded can apply even to how success may ultimately be defined.[18]

Tough Challenge

ECE faces what Adam Kahane would categorize as a tough challenge.[19] The characteristics of tough challenges contrast with problems that can rely on implementing answers based on known knowledge and solutions, regardless of how complicated or demanding to execute. The systemic qualities of tough challenges mean they aren't effectively tackled piece by piece in a sequential fashion. That approach fractures a system into its parts, sidelining the crucial connections and interrelationships upon which a system's cohesion is dependent. Further, their social complexity promotes varied perspectives, values, and interests, requiring those of us living with the challenge to come together and engage in the creative work of resolving it. And because the future being created is as yet undetermined, current "best practices" are rarely capable of offering answers. Instead, new *next practices* have to be created.[20] Finally, ECE's tough challenge has a strong adaptive component, necessitating that as a field we confront new realities, identify gaps between our aspirations and present standing, and grapple with what may need to be discarded in order to evolve into a professional field of practice.[21]

By definition, confronting ECE's tough challenge will entail dealing with uncertainty, disquiet, conflict, and possible loss. Consequently, the change process we're about to undertake involves both our hearts and our minds. As Marty Linsky and Ronald Heifetz noted in their foreword to *Ready or Not: Leadership Choices in Early Care and Education*,[22] inherent to successfully engaging with ECE's tough challenge are

- confronting questions many of us would like to avoid;

- managing resistance, both active and passive, from those of us who have a stake in the status quo; and

- feeling uncomfortable when being held accountable for our role in the challenge at hand as well as for its solutions.

Having become aware of the unpredictable journey ahead, some of us may feel persuaded to withdraw from our field's tough challenge. Yet throughout its history, ECE's aspirations to maximize children's early learning opportunities have inspired our predecessors and colleagues to step forward on the field's behalf. Surely this call for action will arouse similar dedication and commitment.

Changing ECE as a Field of Practice Requires That We Change Ourselves

Our field's beliefs, attitudes, and behaviors have contributed to ECE's past and current challenges. While not solely responsible for ECE's tough challenge, each of us participates in creating and sustaining the systems we now think need to be changed. This realization requires acknowledging that problems "out there" are also "in here"[23] and highlights why professionalizing ECE necessitates different ways of thinking. Few engaged with systems change question that this kind of work depends on new ways of thinking.[24]

Professionalizing Early Childhood Education As a Field of Practice: A Guide to the Next Era begins the field-wide process of seeing and thinking differently about ECE as a field of practice. Innumerable questions await our consideration. For example, at the most basic level, "What unifying purpose brings ECE together across its multiple sectors?" Answers to questions such as this don't already exist, which is what makes our undertaking a tough challenge infused with adaptive work.[25] Moving forward as a professional field of practice, therefore, requires that we open ourselves to change, both individually and collectively. Embracing change is essential to rethinking ECE's occupational configuration for a new era.

> What unifying purpose brings ECE together across its multiple sectors?

HOW DO WE GET STARTED?

Stretching our thinking to escape the field's fragmentation is a primary intent of this book. It may be surprising to learn that the best place to start is with conversations. Not just "any ol' conversations," though, but conversations that engage us in the kind of personal and collective reflection that invites thinking together about how to create an alternative future for ECE.[26] As described by

Juanita Brown, "Conversation is the core process by which we humans think and coordinate our actions together. . . . *Conversation is our human way of creating and sustaining—or transforming—the realities in which we live.*"[27] Conversations with this intent involve three distinct forms: dialogue, discussion, and advocacy. When skillfully practiced, the interplay of these three conversational forms can mobilize new ways of thinking and acting. This makes them ideal for initiating ECE's journey of transformative systems change.

I can imagine eyes rolling! ECE often is criticized for talking too much and using talk as a tactic to avoid taking action. The interactions being launched by this book, though, use conversations as a means for getting to action. Dialogue in conjunction with what Rick Ross and William Isaacs call "skilled discussion" and "balanced advocacy" foster shared understanding and relationship bonds that will be needed for future phases of this work.[28] They also support collaborative learning and generate new best practice possibilities. Specifically, conversations overlaid with intentionality can

- create a different conversational canvas for planning an alternative future for ECE;

- fashion options for realizing ECE as a professional field of practice; and

- lay needed groundwork for what lies ahead.

You're invited to join these conversations so ECE's next era benefits from your knowledge and experience.

ENTERING ECE'S NEXT ERA THROUGH CONVERSATIONS WITH INTENT

This book shepherds the field's entry into a new developmental phase, one that will be fashioned by the field's dedication to realizing ECE's potential, even while necessarily being contoured by current realities. Robert Kegan and Lisa Lahey perhaps best express the dynamic nature of the work ahead: "We must grow into our future possibilities."[29]

The work of restructuring ECE as a field of practice is a tough challenge. Its transformation will not be born from a detailed blueprint or emerge in response to someone driving a predetermined change agenda. Nor would these approaches nurture the ongoing commitment necessary for sustainability.[30] Given ECE's history and current status as a field, transformative action depends first on creating shared understandings, relationships, and intentions.[31]

In addition to the three objectives outlined earlier, these conversations have a fourth objective: to form and foster the conversational skills and boundary-crossing bonds foundational to the development of collective leadership, which, in turn, is integral to effecting systems change.[32] Although the change process is almost guaranteed to be punctuated by uncertainties and anxieties, liberation from outdated habits of mind, shared commitment, and anticipation of ECE's new era will fuel our pioneering work.

Nearly every facet of the field's work is experiencing change. Whether to change is not an option. ECE *will* continue to change. We can step forward as a field of practice and shape what the change looks like or prepare ourselves to be changed by others. Left for us to decide is: Whose vision will drive the field's future?

Three Conversational Forms

As you'll recall, three conversational forms have been identified: dialogue, skilled discussion, and balanced advocacy. These conversational forms can assist the field with examining its mental models and understanding ECE's systemic patterns from multiple perspectives. They also can help generate options for structuring ECE as a professional field of practice.

A systems-thinking term, *mental models* "are deeply ingrained assumptions, generalizations, or even pictures or images that influence how we understand the world and how we take action."[33] When dealing with complex, interdependent issues, individual and collective mental models can often block change. Consequently, guidance offered by this book focuses on increasing self-awareness of our individual and field-wide mental models. Peter Senge, Hal Hamilton, and John Kania identify fostering reflection and generative conversations as a core capability of systems leaders.[34] They also classify creating space for change and enabling the emergence of collective intelligence as one of three core capabilities of system leadership.

Comparing dialogue, skilled discussion, and balanced advocacy can further our understanding of these three conversational forms as well as their contributions to what henceforth will be called conversations with intent.

- *Dialogue* involves a process of reflection and collective inquiry. It differs from other conversational forms by offering a means for creating shared understanding that is born from multiple perspectives on an issue and disentangling the essence of choices. It is founded on (1) slowing down our thinking processes to become more aware of our mental models, (2) asking questions to explore what one doesn't know or understand, and (3) seeking to understand what others see and understand that differs from our point of view. Dialogue takes the energy that comes from understanding different assumptions and channels it toward something never before created.

  The potential for thinking together emerges when our grip loosens on personal positions, allowing new possibilities to emerge, possibilities that might otherwise not have been given the space to develop. In conjunction with skilled discussion, dialogue offers the ECE field a means for going beyond assumptions and beliefs historically saturated with disagreements and imagining new options for achieving common purpose.

- *Skilled discussion* helps dialogue move to action. Typical discussions revolve around sharing one's perspectives, providing an exchange of information. When skilled discussion is used in conjunction with dialogue, however, a conversation can move from exploring underlying causes and assumptions to reaching closure.

  The primary distinction between dialogue and discussion is intention. Dialogue is about exploration, discovery, and insight. Skilled discussion, although reliant on dialogue, shifts conversations toward closure and agreement.

- *Balanced advocacy* involves speaking for one's point of view. When not balanced, it's often associated with a speaker's attempts to persuade others to accept her or his viewpoint and typically presumes the "rightness" of the position being advocated. While change processes require passionate advocates, passion can be polarizing, especially when advocates are not open to rethinking their viewpoints. When a stance excludes those not sharing the position being advocated, others can become defensive and feel pushed into protecting their position rather than opening their minds to explore different views and possibilities.

By opening an assertion's conclusions and assumptions to public testing, though, advocacy can contribute to conversations with intent. When expressed as a clear, calm statement accompanied by the speaker's assumptions, balanced advocacy can help anchor a conversation and contribute to the process of learning from one another. The inherent challenge is tempering advocacy with inquiry.[35]

Getting to Desired Results through Conversations with Intent

When the ECE field began bringing a systemic lens to its work, it often described itself as a nonsystem because of its occupational fragmentation and limited infrastructure. Now more knowledgeable about systems, we realize ECE always has been a system, just not one that can be described as cohesive or as functioning coherently since it lacks binding interconnections that derive from a common function or purpose.

To ensure that last statement was understood, let's make sure each of us knows how a system is defined. A system has three kinds of things: elements, interconnections, and a function or purpose. A nonsystem, therefore, is a conglomeration of things without interconnections or a shared function.[36] An example of a nonsystem would be sand scattered on a road by happenstance and therefore lacking in interconnections and also absent a shared purpose or function.[37]

> A system's behaviors are the result of the structures that created them.

Now compare this example with ECE's configuration as a field of practice: a system of connections disjointed by lack of clarity regarding purpose, identity, or responsibility.[38] Finally, compare these last two examples with professional fields of practice: interconnected and interdependent systems of preparation, practice, and accountability bound together by common purpose.

As systems thinkers, we are learning that a system's behaviors result from the structures that created them. Often invisible, systemic structures are patterns of interconnections among a system's key elements. As Donella Meadows puts it, "The behavior of a system cannot be known just by knowing the elements of which the system is made."[39]

These insights help us recognize that ECE's fragmented status as a field of practice, underdeveloped workforce, and uneven promotion of learning and development in early learning settings result from the way in which the field's systemic elements are interconnected. The current connections among ECE's systemic elements are clearly not well serving children, families, or society.

> Current connections among ECE's systemic elements are clearly not well serving children, families, or society.

ECE has always been a system. There always have been connections among its parts, but their interrelationships no longer are adequate in the context of the field's new realities. *Only restructuring the current system* can remedy the consequences being experienced by the field and those dependent upon it.[40] Organizing ECE as a professional field of practice restructures ECE's current occupational configuration, allowing the field's tough challenge to be tackled at a systemic level responsive to its complexity.

ABOUT THIS BOOK

I think *Professionalizing Early Childhood Education As a Field of Practice: A Guide to the Next Era* has the potential to be historically meaningful for ECE as a field of practice. Throughout its history in the United States—using the kindergarten movement as my marker for the onset of ECE as a field of practice—ECE has evolved haphazardly. Sheldon White and Steve Buka described the field's development prior to the creation of Head Start as a research and development sequence.[41] Different versions of ECE emerged from practical needs, private and government projects, and insights from philosophy, educational ideologies, and utopian programs. Since Head Start, the field's evolution has been characterized by expanding programs and policies, galvanized then, as now, by the potential for social change. Bernard Spodek and Herbert Walberg called this period an era of abundance.[42] Then in the 1990s, driven by the field's expansion, particularly the growing numbers of children in child care, systems development took precedence over program development. Now, twenty-five years later, the ECE field is still grappling with creating systems that meaningfully affect the caliber of children's early learning experiences.

This is not the first time the question of professionalizing ECE as a field of practice has arisen,[43] but this does seem to be the first time the question is getting traction. Anointing this book with historical significance likely overstates the moment. Yet it's nonetheless noteworthy that for the first time the field is expressing an openness to confronting the gap between its aspirations and its current realities. There appears to be growing willingness to acknowledge that the systems changes ahead require making hard choices that to date have largely been evaded. This may truly be a defining moment for ECE as a field of practice.

Entering Uncharted Water

ECE has become typified by its outward focus: building public awareness and expanding public and policy support to address the systemic consequences of its explosive growth and to plug weaknesses increasingly being magnified, as limitations of the field's current occupational structure are revealed in the face of new realities. Yet despite massive efforts and investments since the 1990s directed toward building statewide ECE systems, consequential change has been elusive. The time has come for an inward focus and effecting change from inside out.[44]

Early educators' crucial role in effecting children's positive learning and development has been empirically confirmed. It's no longer possible to ignore the negative consequences stemming from inconsistencies in practitioners' knowledge and skills. The ECE field needs to step forward, act on its convictions, and engage with what should be *its* work: structuring ECE as a profession capable of preparing and supporting practitioners who consistently contribute to children's optimum learning and development regardless of setting, sponsor, or funding stream.

The journey begins with conversations that explore possibilities for restructuring ECE, confronting choices that await us, and moving forward. This book presents questions along with guidance for conversations with the intention of creating shared meaning to inform an alternative future for ECE as a professional field of practice. By offering an approach for transcending fragmented thinking and enabling ECE's outlines as a profession to emerge, *conversations with intent will launch the field's first collective action in service to restructuring ECE as a field of practice.*

> The journey begins with conversations that explore possibilities . . .

Collective leadership will be required to structure ECE as a profession. While we can learn from other professions' experiences, ECE is entering into uncharted territory. As a starting point, we need to become more deeply aware of the systems of which we are a part. We also must develop dispositions and skills for engaging with colleagues to imagine an alternative future for ECE.

Engaging with Systems-Defining Questions

The work starts with scrutinizing our individual and field-wide mental models. By changing our mental models, we can alter our relationship to change.[45] By expanding our grasp of systemic relationship possibilities, we extend our potential to think differently. Simultaneously, conversations with intent will ripen the field's readiness to move beyond the status quo.[46] While an increasing number of us endorse the need to restructure ECE's present configuration, its urgency has yet to be recognized by the ECE field as a whole.

This book steers the field's collective inquiry toward five overarching questions whose answers are fundamental to advancing ECE as a professional field of practice:

1. What major choices will be required to move ECE forward as a profession? Are we prepared as a field of practice to make those choices?

2. What principles or values should guide the formation of ECE as a professional field of practice?

3. What options are available for ECE's structure as a professional field of practice?

4. What should be the starting place(s) for structuring ECE as a profession?

5. What else do we need to know to move forward? Who else can we be learning from?

HOW TO USE THIS BOOK

This first chapter has summarized both the reasoning and need for moving ECE into its next era. It identifies the field's tough challenge and why addressing it matters. It explains why conversations with intent should be the field's first step toward developing a shared agenda for systems change.

Yet the conversations promoted by this book will succeed only if we remember that the three conversational forms I'm advocating differ from our usual forms of conversing. They are designed to foster insights into the tough challenge we are trying to solve and to accelerate the availability of actionable knowledge.

Chapter 2, Thinking Alone, invites us to begin our preparation with internally oriented questions directed toward developing awareness of our mental models:

- how we as individuals are contributing to ECE's system as it now exists;

- how we may inadvertently be blocking our and others' openness to different ways of thinking; and

- priming us for participation in systemically oriented conversations geared toward generating new possibilities.

Deeper self-knowledge and openness to others' thinking will broaden our understanding of ECE as a field of practice. This much-needed expansion of understanding comes from opening ourselves to other's perspectives, concerns, and aspirations for our field. Conversation by conversation, newly forged insights and exploration of different possibilities will create an entryway into future deliberations and decision making. Integral to this next step is forging consensus that, *yes, the time has arrived for coming together as a field to structure ECE as an organized profession. And yes, we will join together on a scale commensurate with our challenge and commit to serving something larger than ourselves.*

As already noted, this is not the first time the question of professionalizing ECE has arisen, although perhaps never quite so directly.[47] Are we willing to confront our individual and collective biases about ECE as a field of practice? Are we capable of joining together to coevolve a different reality for ECE? Are we ready to steer ECE toward a future in line with its potential? The purpose of conversations with intent is to probe our thinking in ways that set the stage for collective creativity and action. The questions presented in chapter 2 (Thinking Alone) will help you examine your personal beliefs and values, the locale of your resistance to change, and your fears for what may be lost, personally and as a field. By engaging with these questions prior to coming together with colleagues to explore questions posed in chapter 3, you will contribute to making these conversations far richer and more productive.

Formally structuring ECE as a profession will prompt trepidations,[48] and exploring these concerns is essential to building internal cohesion, surfacing fresh possibilities, and sustaining the trajectory set for ECE's future. The questions posed in chapter 3, Thinking Together, attempt to bring our diverse, and often divisive, views to the forefront. As Heifetz alerts us, clarifying what matters most, in what balance, and with what trade-offs will be a central task of our work.[49]

The final chapter, Supporting Successful Conversations with Intent, offers suggestions related to convening, hosting, and facilitating conversations with intent. For readers interested in deepening their expertise beyond what is offered here, resources are identified in the chapter note attached to this sentence.[50]

This book is relevant and timely for a wide audience. It will be of special interest to readers and conversation participants who will experience the greatest change in role and responsibilities once ECE professionalizes. This includes teachers who on a daily basis interact with children in early learning settings, administrators who create working conditions supportive of effective practice, and others such as higher education faculty, trainers, and professional development providers who promote the knowledge, skills, and dispositions essential to teachers' and administrators' competence.

Individuals in any of these roles can also convene groups to explore the questions outlined in chapter 3. Already, individuals in these various roles are convening study groups or engaging colleagues at their places of work or at state and local meetings. Other conversation hosts, although not limited to them, include the field's prominent national associations and their affiliated organizations.

Yes, courage and risk-taking will be required for the work ahead. Yet bypassing this call to restructure ECE as a field of practice would mean forsaking ECE's obligations to children, families, and itself as a field of practice. Heifetz would likely label this choice *resistance to change* or *work avoidance*.[51]

I'm hoping this interpretation is mistaken. The next step is ours to take. Shall we start the conversation?

Thinking Alone

ECE IS UNDERPERFORMING as a field of practice. Since the mid-1990s, attention has focused on building an ECE system capable of offering positive early learning experiences to the growing number of children in programs, especially those children experiencing gaps in their early learning and development. Yet as the field's footprint has expanded and the societal value placed on high-caliber ECE programs has grown, systemic weaknesses have become more visible, leading to increasing pressure to reform ECE as a field of practice.

This chapter returns to a crucial point made in chapter 1: Each of us involved with ECE is part of the system we want to change. By structuring ECE as a professional field of practice with interconnected systems of preparation, practice, and accountability tightly bound by common purpose, we can become more competent as early learning practitioners. The systems changes required to bring this vision to fruition, though, depend on the exercise of collective leadership.

Collective leadership is exercised through the actions of individuals who join together to effect change. ECE's transformation as a field of practice needs to involve each of us, which means we each will need to step forward and continually expand the circle of individuals participating in conversations with intent. For many of us, this will require what may be new skills.

> Each of us involved with ECE is part of the system we want to change.

For the "whole system" of ECE to be understood, families, policy makers, and other decision makers will at some point need to be brought into our conversations. Yet conversations with intent should start with us if as a field of practice we're going to step forward to exercise collective leadership on ECE's behalf.

This chapter begins by underlining the importance of attending to our mental models—the underlying assumptions forming our worldview—when restructuring systems. Then questions are presented for probing our personal assumptions. By definition, assumptions are conjectures or hypotheses. When part of our mental models, though, they often are perceived as accepted truths, "truths" to which we can become very loyal.

WE ARE PART OF THE SYSTEM WE WANT TO CHANGE

ECE's uneven performance as a field of practice is a result of its current structure. As Donella Meadows explains, "No one deliberately creates those problems, no one wants them to persist, but they persist nonetheless. That is because they are intrinsically systems problems—undesirable behaviors characteristic of the system structures that produce them. They will yield only as we reclaim our intuition, stop casting blame, see the system as the source of its own problems, and find the courage and wisdom to *restructure* it."[1]

Technical solutions to ECE's tough challenge will have limited impact because ECE's problematic situation is deeply rooted in the internal structure of the field's current occupational configuration. As Michael Fullan has argued in his assessment of education reform efforts, striving for policy, structural, and procedural alignment are inadequate to the problem. While having a role in education's "reform constellation," they are ineffective for tackling whole system reform because they "alter structure, procedures and other formal attributes of the system without reaching the internal substance of reform."[2]

· ·

Are we ready to be part of the solution?

· ·

ECE can address its "internal substance of reform" by restructuring its occupational configuration and organizing as a professional field of practice. Admittedly, restructuring ECE will be neither swift nor easy. It will be an unfolding process, one that is often simultaneously messy, anxiety provoking, and exhilarating. Coming together to create an alternative future for ECE is a tremendous opportunity.

The necessity of acting on choices that involve potential loss defines the work ahead as adaptive. The presence of dynamic, social, and generative complexity (described in chapter 1) identifies it as a tough challenge. The chance to move beyond problem solving to establish a new direction for our field marks it as a transformative opportunity.[3] We have the energizing prospect of changing the future by structuring ECE as a professional field of practice.

Transitioning from "being a part of the problem" to "being a part of the solution" depends on increasing self-awareness of our mental models and opening up to alternative ways of understanding. This will require developing and testing new mental models. This applies to us both as individuals and as a field of practice. Charlotte Roberts maintains that revising mental models offers the highest leverage for change.[4] As expressed by Adam Kahane, "We bring (a different future) about through transforming our own thoughts and actions and our relationships with others."[5]

The process begins with personal reflection and inquiry into our ideas and beliefs: slowing down our thinking so we can become more aware of our mental models and how they were formed; holding up the mirror to recognize the taken-for-granted assumptions we carry into conversations; and acknowledging that our mental models may be restricting our worldview. This is difficult work, though, because it requires us to

- reflect and inquire into our thoughts, emotions, and everyday behaviors;

- delve into the source of beliefs underlying our actions; and

- sometimes unearth uncomfortable discoveries.

Professionalizing ECE, therefore, involves a developmental process not only for the field but also for each of us as individuals. By becoming aware of our "self-authoring minds,"[6] we open ourselves to developing what Kegan and Lahey call "increasingly sophisticated levels of mental complexity."[7] Thus, each of us is being asked to explore assumptions that may be blocking us from considering different possibilities. "They are not so much the assumptions we have," Kegan and Lahey contend, "as they are assumptions *that have us*."[8] These assumptions maintain the status quo by

- appearing automatically without intention or awareness;

- being viewed as accepted truths;

- creating a sense of certainty that our worldview is reality; and

- anchoring and sustaining our equilibrium.[9]

Sometimes we hold our assumptions so deeply, we identify with them.[10] We typically avoid confronting our assumptions, though, because of the discomfort it creates. This commonly is labeled as *resistance to change*. Our resistance alerts us to the possible presence of an adaptive challenge—our being put face-to-face with values at odds with one another, being challenged with having to possibly prioritize what we hold dear, and then feeling anxiety about what might be lost as a result. Consequently, a solid commitment to self-development is essential. Awareness of how and why we may react to another's thinking in particular ways needs to be fostered so we can be open to different perspectives and increase self-awareness of how we inhibit or facilitate diverse views.

It follows that emotional responses sometimes accompany the work we're about to undertake. It's one thing to intellectually accept different viewpoints; it's another to expose our assumptions publicly. In a conversational setting, for example, our views may be shown to be flawed or incomplete, prompting feelings of embarrassment or discomfort. So in addition to learning to take deep breaths to still instantaneous emotional reactions, it's important to distinguish our role from who we are as a person.

Most of us put our hearts and souls into the work we do with and on behalf of children and their families. Still, our work role is not the same as who we are as individuals. Participants in your conversations with intent may know you in your work-related role. They may or may not know you personally, and if they do, perhaps only superficially. Even if someone criticizes you in order to divert attention from a contentious issue, recognizing you're not being attacked personally can reduce your sense of vulnerability and allow you to deflect personal comments and stay focused on what is happening or needs to happen in the conversation.[11]

QUESTIONS FOR SELF-REFLECTION

How you engage in reflective practice is your choice to make. Like any activity, the more you invest in it, the more you'll get out of it—and in this instance, the more you'll also be able to contribute to conversations with intent and explore possibilities for structuring ECE as a professional field of practice.

Some of the questions presented are original in their conception; others are adapted from a variety of sources, all of which can be found in the References list.[12] All are worded to the extent possible to align with the conceptualization of ECE's tough challenge and the principles of system, collective, and adaptive leadership. Questions intentionally overlap, offering different entry points for reflection. Spaces are provided for inserting your thoughts directly into this document. You might also want to consider starting a separate journal to help organize your thoughts. Be aware that this exercise is not a "one-night assignment." These are questions to mull over time.

The sheer number of questions may feel overwhelming. Choose those questions you find most interesting, and feel free to choose the order in which you think about them. Try, though, to contemplate questions from each of the four topics.

> The more you invest in reflective practice, the more you'll get out of it.

- Assumptions Behind My ECE Actions

- Commitment to Personal Change

- Openness to Changing ECE as a Field of Practice

- Conversational Skills

Then, because this exercise is about expanding self-knowledge, you might want to give thought as to why you are bypassing certain questions. Was it only about what you found interesting or the time you had available for personal reflection? Could there instead be an underlying mindset to your choices? Is there a pattern to the questions you are avoiding?

Importantly, these are *your* thoughts. You need not share your answers with anyone unless you choose to do so. Remember that our thoughts are inventions.[13] They almost always are incomplete. Why? Because it's not humanly possible to know everything necessary to fully understand a system as complex as ECE as a field of practice. This explains why being exposed to diverse perspectives is so important to conversations about professionalizing ECE as a field of practice and why conversations with intent promise to be mind-expanding.

To support your reflective process, you might consider the following:

1. Naming your assumptions

2. Asking yourself where the assumption came from—how did it come to be

3. Exploring the consequences of the assumption on your behavior, your

interactions with colleagues, and your thoughts about ECE as a field of practice

4. Asking what would happen if you loosened your hold on the assumption

Assumptions Behind My ECE Actions

These questions will help you examine how your thinking and actions may be sustaining or contributing to the field's status quo behavior.

1. What is my personal stake in restructuring ECE as a field of practice?

_____

_____

_____

2. Am I acting in ways consistent with the values I espouse as an early educator?

_____

_____

_____

3. What am I doing in my work role that possibly maintains ECE's current inability to consistently provide high quality early learning experiences (even when not the intent)?

_____

_____

_____

Commitment to Personal Change

These questions focus on your openness to change and willingness to engage with new possibilities for restructuring ECE as a field of practice.

4. How committed am I to changing? What evidence do I have that I'm open to change?

    _____

    _____

    _____

5. What values or thinking about ECE as a field of practice feel "untouchable"?

    _____

    _____

    _____

6. What makes me feel so sure I'm right about my "certainties"?

    _____

    _____

    _____

7. What would be placed at risk if I let go of my "certainties"? What am I afraid of losing? How might I test my assumption(s) in this regard?

    _____

    _____

    _____

8. Do I have unspoken commitments to colleagues, staff, or families that are holding me back from rethinking my perspective on X? Can I identify examples where my unspoken commitments have influenced my behavior?

    _____

    _____

    _____

9. Do I have a personal agenda/ambition that I'm allowing to trump a new agenda for ECE as a field of practice? If so, what is it? How is it affecting my reactions to a change agenda?

_____

_____

_____

10. In order to fully engage and learn, how much of myself am I willing to reveal so I can get the benefits of how others view my ideas?

_____

_____

_____

11. To whom or what am I being loyal? Who would react most strongly if I did something differently? Is this preventing me from changing?

_____

_____

_____

12. Am I willing to be influenced by the conversations being planned? Why or why not?

_____

_____

_____

Openness to Changing ECE as a Field of Practice

These questions probe your commitment to ECE's present configuration as a field of practice and readiness to engage with others in co-creating a different future for ECE as a field of practice.

13. What are my aspirations for ECE as a field of practice? What is it I really want to create?

_____

_____

_____

14. When in conversation about ECE's need to change, what gives me "butterflies in my stomach"? Why?

_____

_____

_____

15. Am I getting in the way of advancing ECE as a professional field of practice? If so, in what ways?

_____

_____

_____

16. How committed am I to creating an alternative future for ECE as a field of practice?

_____

_____

_____

17. What questions do I have that don't yet have answers? What questions do I want to learn more about?

_____

_____

_____

18. What does ECE's future as a field of practice need from me?

_____

_____

_____

Conversational Skills

In preparation for your conversational interactions, the next questions explore how you engage with others during inquiry-oriented and sometimes difficult conversations.

19. How do I tend to respond when I am feeling vulnerable? What do these responses and vulnerabilities tell me about myself?

_____

_____

_____

20. How do I think others see me? How might this influence my willingness to expose my thinking during conversations?

_____

_____

_____

21. What are my default reactions? What triggers my "hot buttons"?

_____

_____

_____

22. How do I express resistance when responding to ideas I find disagreeable?

_____

_____

_____

23. What do I need to feel or do to be fully engaged and energized by conversations with intent?

_____

_____

_____

CHAPTER 3

Thinking Together

AS ROBERT FRITZ underscores, "We have been trained to think of situations that are inadequate for our aspirations as problems. When we think of them as problems, you are taking action to have something go away: *the problem*. When you are creating, you are taking action to have something come into being: *the creation*."[1] This distinction forms the basis for conversations with intent.

Conversations aren't typically characterized as agents for change. Increasingly, though, they are becoming recognized as powerful sources of creativity, shared wisdom, and generative possibility that can be channeled to bring alternative futures into existence.[2] This makes them ideal as a starting point for our shared journey. *Professionalizing Early Childhood Education As a Field of Practice: A Guide to the Next Era* steers our collective inquiry and creativity toward five overarching questions whose answers are fundamental to creating ECE as a professional field of practice:

1. What major choices will be required to move ECE forward as a profession? Are we prepared as a field of practice to make them?

2. What principles or values should guide formation of ECE as a professional field of practice?

3. What options are available for ECE's organization as a professional field of practice?

4. What should be the starting place(s) for structuring ECE as a profession?

5. What else do we need to know to move forward? Who else should we be learning from?

These questions require thinking that goes beyond what any single one of us could conjure up on our own. Plus, as William Isaacs highlights in his description of dialogue, "We need to make a collective shift as well as an individual one. This means learning to think with others and not merely on our own."[3] Conversations with intent launch the field's first collective action in service to restructuring ECE as a field of practice. These five overarching questions are intended to unleash our collective inquiry and creativity as well as deepen our commitments to ECE's next era.

SETTING THE STAGE FOR CONVERSATIONS WITH INTENT

At this juncture in the field's developmental journey, conversations with intent aren't about pursuing agreement. They are for the purpose of creating formative pools of shared understanding that can inform future field-wide actions. So regardless of their location, it is important that they stay connected to their purpose: deepening understanding of ECE as a field of practice and exploring options for its evolution to a professional field of practice. As the means for elevating the caliber of our pedagogical practices and universalizing them among early educators, professionalizing ECE can alter the quality and effectiveness of children's formal early learning experiences regardless of program sector, setting, sponsor, or funding stream.

> Conversations with intent launch the first collective action toward restructuring ECE as a field of practice.

The nature of ECE's tough challenge is best addressed by shifting from a problem-solving orientation to one focused on creating a compelling future for ECE as a field of practice and designing a system that brings the field's desired behaviors to fruition. As the first chapter outlined, conversations with intent, characterized by the interplay of dialogue, skilled discussion, and advocacy balanced with inquiry, can assist the ECE field with examining its mental models, understanding systemic patterns from multiple perspectives, and generating options for ECE as a professional field of practice. Two fundamentals are required to bring this about: meaningful questions and skills for maximizing the potential available from the interplay among these three conversational forms.

Questions function as instruments for change by influencing what we think about together.[4] Their purpose when part of conversations with intent is to foster expression of multiple viewpoints, move us beyond the field's segmented "parts" to foster conceptualization of ECE as a whole, and prompt collective inquiry and creativity. What can ensue are new ways of seeing the field's realities that, in turn, prompt fresh and sometimes novel possibilities for consideration. In addition to trust in the process, realizing this potential requires different conversational skills than those used during routine conversations or during debate and typical advocacy.

FOUNDATIONAL PRACTICES

It helps to remember that dialogue and skilled discussion are primarily about introspection and inquiry. They ask us to question our certainties and bypass temptations to jump into a problem-solving mode. Suspending our thoughts opens us to the possibility that our thinking may, in fact, not be as right as we think, and in the process creates space for deeper understanding and new possibilities to emerge.

Three interconnected practices are repeatedly highlighted as essential to establishing conditions for effective conversations with intent: listening, respecting, and suspending. They are applicable to us as individual participants and as a conversation group.

- *Listening* involves attending to others and also listening to our reactions to what is being said. It requires distinguishing what is being said from our almost instantaneous interpretation of what we're hearing. It demands we quiet our inner noise and focus our attention so we can hear the meaning speakers are trying to convey while at the same time being conscious of our inner responses.

- *Respecting* goes beyond being polite and allowing speakers to finish their sentences. It is the act of accepting what a speaker has to say as a legitimate perspective even if we personally disagree with what's being expressed. In the context of what these conversations are intended to accomplish, respect involves trying to understand the source of another's point of view without interjecting to explain why it's wrong or doesn't make sense. This practice is core to understanding thinking and feelings that sustain different interpretations of the same phenomenon and to recognizing our thinking as but one possibility within a greater whole, even if, ultimately, our existing beliefs remain unchanged.

- *Suspending* involves restraining the usual response of resisting a different opinion or defending our own. We observe our reactions to others' thinking without feeling compelled to express them, creating space for personal and collective inquiry and the emergence of new insights. Think of the act of suspending as hanging an assumption in the middle of the room for all (including those with the assumption) to question and explore.[5]

Three additional underpinnings of these conversations warrant our attention:

- Participants can play different roles during conversations.[6] These roles perform identifiable functions, each differently facilitating dialogue and skilled discussion. See Conversational Roles for a description of these roles and functions.

- While in the midst of a conversation, it's often helpful to "get up on the balcony."[7] Metaphorically accomplished by an individual participant or by the group as a whole, one mentally removes himself or herself from the conversation underway to observe and gather perspective on oneself and the system in the room: "What's happening here and what is my role in what's occurring?" The balcony perspective helps inform interpretations about the dynamics in the room, viewpoints being expressed, and the extent to which patterns may be emerging. The more interpretations we have, the more capable we will be in making sense of what's going on in the room and understanding ECE as a system.

- Different perspectives are good, even when they provoke tension or conflict.[8] Disagreements reveal the need to dig deeper for understanding. They create openings for investigating differences and exploring multiple options. When experienced as conflict, they may indicate an adaptive challenge, suggesting that a value or belief is being threatened, even if the speaker is unaware of expressing emotional discomfort.

Sometimes "raising the temperature" during a conversation can be a tactic to create sufficient disequilibrium to spur questioning of prevalent assumptions and motivate exploration of other possibilities.[9] An optimal level of conflict challenges the limits of our current way of understanding something we care about. Under the best of circumstances, it neither overwhelms us nor allows the issue to be ignored.[10]

The three foundational practices of conversations with intent are played out in myriad small ways, as are the three more advanced understandings just described. Under the header Boosting Our Contributions to the Group Conversation, suggestions are offered for incorporating these practices into your repertoire.

At this point, it may feel less daunting to think of conversations with intent as collaborative conversations. Competency with these foundational and more advanced skills obviously develop fully only after repeated practice. Sharing them here, though, allows us to acknowledge that dialogue, skilled discussion, and advocacy balanced by inquiry are distinctive conversational forms bolstered by familiarity with their specialized "tools." Further, these skills will need to become widely known and practiced if the field is to exercise collective leadership on behalf of ECE's future.

> **CONVERSATIONAL ROLES[1]**
>
> Participants can play different roles at different times during a conversation. Each of the roles listed below can contribute to generating the expanded intelligence and creativity desired from conversations with intent. Notice that the four roles are labeled using terms indicating that participants in these roles are actively engaged with the interaction of which they are a part.
>
> - *Bystanding*: the participant makes comments about the process but not content.
> - *Sensing*: the participant watches the conversation flow without saying much yet is very aware of what's transpiring and presents interpretations for others to consider.
> - *Clarifying*: the participant poses questions that lead to clarification about what is being discussed, for example, "What is the question we're trying to answer?"
> - *Interviewing*: the participant explores others' points of views and the reasons behind them.

BOOSTING OUR CONTRIBUTIONS TO THE GROUP CONVERSATION

As part of our preparations for conversations with intent, we've become aware that perceived truths are actually assumptions. You have probed your individual mental models and sensitized yourself to some of your presumptions. Now you're likely curious to learn what your colleagues are thinking.

Our preparations aren't yet quite complete, though. Without losing what you've learned about yourself and perhaps some new thinking about ECE as a field of practice, we now need to consider how individually and together we can maximize the potential of conversations with intent to carry us into the future we want to create for ECE. We want to prepare for a different way of being together. If we enter conversations with in-

We want to prepare for a different way of being together.

tent ready to practice what we're learning, deepened relationships, fresh thinking, and optimism for ECE's future are more likely to result.

To facilitate this outcome, below are (1) Keep in Minds, suggestions for how to be present in the conversation, and (2) Questions to Facilitate Meaningful Dialogue, language for fostering meaningful conversations with intent. While what follows offers some new skills, just as often it is intended to help you recall what's already been described.

Keep in Minds

- Remember Shared Reflection and Inquiry Are the Purpose of Dialogue
  - Acknowledge your contribution to the field's tough challenge.
  - Hold your views as hypotheses.
    - Describe ECE's present condition or circumstance as you see them, without offering judgment.
    - Consider how others may interpret your comments.
    - Build on ideas that are being expressed.
  - Give speakers opportunity to complete their thoughts.
  - Be present to what is happening and to your reactions.
  - Avoid being judgmental. Don't blame others for "what is" or attack a view you don't hold.
  - Be willing to suspend your view. Conflicts are inevitable when you hold on to your certainties and others in the room do the same.
  - Allow different points of view to live alongside one another. Sidestep debating them or explaining why you think they're wrong.
  - Avoid self-censorship. If you choose to remain silent, try becoming aware of what stopped you by later recalling the story you told yourself to maintain your silence.
  - Be comfortable with pauses and quiet—yours and others—when it indicates careful listening, thinking, or reflection.

o Be attentive to others in the room whose thoughts aren't being expressed. Try inviting them to speak or try saying what you're sensing needs to be expressed so it can be considered by others.

o Feel comfortable with "raising the temperature" in the room if you think it will help expose underlying assumptions or values.

o Try speaking "to the center" instead of to another person in the room. This minimizes interpersonal dynamics and facilitates creation of a shared pool of understanding.

o Similarly, try listening together as a group.

o Focus on what's possible. Redirect conversation blaming external forces for hindering change; focus instead on examining what the field can do differently.

o If transitioning the conversation from dialogue to skilled discussion, identify the shift you are making.[11]

- Use Questions to Explore Underlying Meaning and Assumptions

  o Avoid asking questions with obvious answers or masking a bias. Open-ended questions typically start with words like *how, what, which,* or *why.*[12]

  o Instead of advocating for an idea, put out a question for exploration.

- Be Prepared for the Unexpected

  o Don't personalize what's being said. Remember our thoughts are assumptions. Separate your *role* from *who you are as a person.*

  o Be prepared for defensive responses. They are to be expected. Structuring ECE as a professional field of practice will rearrange existing relationships, and some proposals might directly affect us or challenge closely held beliefs. Conversations with intent, therefore, can feel very personal for some of us. While it's important to be sensitive to this feature of adaptive change, remember that if the temperature in the room is not raised *too* high, tension can catalyze new insights and ways of thinking.

  o Name and acknowledge fears, your own as well as others, but don't give in to them.

o Look for and name value conflicts embedded in different viewpoints, what and whose interests benefit from the status quo, and political dynamics that sustain the current situation.[13]

Questions to Facilitate Meaningful Dialogue

Questions and phrases that can facilitate effective dialogue are shared below. They are organized by three overarching categories: (1) Deepening Understanding of Underlying Thinking, (2) Expanding the Exploration Underway, and (3) Lowering the Room Temperature.

- Deepening Understanding of Underlying Thinking
    - o Can you please explain a bit more about X?
    - o What's missing from the conversation thus far? What is it we're not seeing?
    - o Is there another way of understanding what's being expressed?
    - o Can you say more so I can better understand the assumptions or beliefs embedded in your question/statement?
    - o That's an interesting thought. Where does it come from? What is it based on?
    - o What in your experience leads you to that response?
    - o Why do you think that thought is important?
    - o What in our conversation thus far isn't receiving sufficient attention?
    - o What do you see as the difference between X and Y?
    - o What is the concern you're trying to speak to?
    - o Do you believe that means . . . ?
- Expanding the Exploration Underway
    - o What are some deeper questions we could ask to extend our understanding of ECE as a field of practice?
    - o How can the ideas being explored elevate ECE's competence as a field of practice?
    - o What might be some hidden issues in this conversation that are impeding our collective learning?

- o How will your thoughts help us better understand our assumptions and advance ECE as a professional field of practice? What is the question we're trying to answer?

- o What about ECE as presently configured may be enabling what you're describing?

- o Here's my synthesis of what I think we've said thus far. What do you think?

- o How else might we look at this?

- o Is there an interest group missing from our conversation? How might it respond to the issue we're exploring?

- o I'm not sure where our conversation is going. Can someone help me?

- o Are there underlying patterns to the different views being expressed?

- o Are those of us in the room experiencing different emotional reactions to what's being said? Have we perhaps tapped into something important that we need to further understand?

- Lowering the Room Temperature: If despite the best of intentions, it feels as if the tone of the conversation is becoming uncomfortably strained, the following language possibilities may help defuse tensions.

  - o What I heard you say that I appreciated is . . .

  - o What I heard that challenged my thinking is . . .

  - o To better understand your perspective, I'd like to ask you . . .

  - o When a conversation feels gridlocked: How big a deal is this?

  - o In response to detours: acknowledge the observation and then ask the speaker to reframe the comment so it speaks to the issue at hand.

  - o To redirect the conversation when you, rather than your idea, has become the focus: I think this is an issue for all of us, or Given the purpose of our conversation . . .

CREATING SHARED MEANING ABOUT ECE AS A PROFESSIONAL FIELD OF PRACTICE

We've reached the moment to apply our knowledge and skills about effective conversations with intent to questions pertinent to structuring ECE as a profession. Remember to keep these conversations connected to our purpose: professionalizing ECE as a field of practice so that systemic capacity exists to consistently promote children's optimum learning and development. As John Goodlad noted for us, "A vocation is not a profession just because those in it choose to call it one. It must be recognized as such."[14] To help us keep this in mind, Characteristics of Professional Fields of Practice identify the criteria ECE will have to address to be recognized as a profession.

CHARACTERISTICS OF PROFESSIONAL FIELDS OF PRACTICE

Professions are coherent, interconnected systems of preparation, practice, and accountability.[1]

They are characterized by

- clarity of shared purpose or function;
- identification of who's "in" the field and who's not;
- organizing structures and supportive institutions that unify the field and its practitioners through common knowledge, skills, and dispositions;
- clear scopes and standards of practice;
- responsibility for evolving and applying a specialized knowledge base;
- ethical responsibility to perform at consistent levels of competence and assume responsibility for results; and
- proactive leadership to facilitate field-wide adaptation to new circumstances, capture opportunities for improving practice, and advocate for conditions that make competent practice possible and accessible.[2]

Peter Senge cites Humberto Maturana as saying, "History follows the path of our desires."[15] He interpreted this quote as inviting us to "assume responsibility we usually shirk."[16] While obviously not limited solely to what we do, ECE's future hinges on what we choose to do as a field of practice. The contributions our field makes to children, families, and society is at stake. ECE's potential as a professional field of practice depends on the choices we choose to enact.

Questions to Support Co-creation of ECE as a Professional Field of Practice

Some of the questions shared below are original in their conception; others are adapted from a variety of sources, all of which can be found in the References list.[17] To the extent possible, all are aligned with the characteristics of powerful questions,[18] my conceptualization of ECE's tough challenge, and principles associated with system, collective, and adaptive leadership. You'll note that I have not included questions related to compensation. I support the high priority placed on worthy wages. Before this crucial issue can be thoughtfully tackled, though, ECE as a field of practice needs to define its unique contribution to society, identify its specialized knowledge base, and establish its performance expectations. Our conclusions will provide the basis for creating an equitable compensation system that is aligned with qualifications, role responsibilities, and societal recognition of the field's value.

Spaces are provided for inserting your initial thinking directly into this document. As suggested in chapter 2, you might instead want to use a journal to record your initial thinking. Additionally, a journal could be used to track your group's discussion.

You may recall seeing some of these same questions, or a variation of them, in chapter 2. When this occurs, it's because the question is as pertinent to probing assumptions held by ECE as a field of practice as they are to understanding our individual mental models. Questions may also sometimes appear overlapping or redundant; this occurs when issues have varied entry points for exploration.

> **ECE's future hinges on what we choose to do as a field of practice.**

The questions, with the exception of those organized under the final topical heading, can inform the five overarching questions guiding conversations with intent. For organizational purposes, questions are arranged by four topic headings:

I. ECE's Mental Models as a Field of Practice

II. Structuring ECE as a Professional Field of Practice

III. Co-creating ECE as a Professional Field of Practice

IV. Questions for Shared Reflection

The number of possible questions far exceeds what can be meaningfully explored during a single or even multiple conversations. Explore those questions you and your colleagues care about most; their sequence is yours to choose. They are not arranged in any specific order or hierarchy. Ideally, the same questions will continue to be explored over time, deepening individual and shared understanding over several conversations.

You are encouraged, though, to explore questions from each of the first three categories. Doing so will support inquiry into systemic issues pertinent to structuring ECE as a profession.

Because it can be hard to set aside the possibility of personal impact as a result of changing ECE as a field of practice, conversations with intent may be aided by the group's up-front agreement to (1) assume ECE has experienced a tsunami and is rebuilding itself from scratch and (2) set a date into the future for the rebuilding to be completed. This can help depersonalize the conversation and reduce feelings of being personally threatened by potential change.[19]

Finally, the assemblage of these questions makes evident the scope of our quest. Remember, though, what has been learned from occupations that have organized themselves as professions: We are at the start of an extended developmental journey. We aren't expected to know all of the answers up front.

ECE's journey requires us to forge a shared commitment to fulfilling a common purpose, identify our field's unique contribution to society's well-being, determine the field's specialized expertise, and navigate currents of the field's social and economic context. Personalizing Senge and his colleagues' forecast first shared in chapter 1, "Like others before us, we will discover much of the plot as we invent it."[20]

I. ECE's Mental Models as a Field of Practice

These questions focus on our underlying assumptions about ECE as a field of practice, highlighting sources of our field's fragmentation and illuminating possibilities for finding common purpose in the context of new realities.

1. What are ECE's unquestioned assumptions? Why are these assumptions so tightly held? What would be at risk if they were let go? What are some of us afraid the field might lose?

    _____

    _____

    _____

2. What are assumptions we hold about ECE's different sectors?

    _____

    _____

    _____

3. What is the cost to ECE of maintaining the same path, tinkering around the edges as we go?[21]

_____

_____

_____

4. What is emerging as ECE's future if we don't step forward to create an alternative trajectory?

_____

_____

_____

5. What are ECE's new realities calling for it to become?

_____

_____

_____

6. What of ECE's past and present is most important to preserve? Do new values need to be embraced? If so, what might they be?

_____

_____

_____

7. What is not receiving sufficient attention as a field of practice? Why might that be?

_____

_____

_____

8. What behaviors are preventing ECE from moving forward as a field of practice?

_____

_____

_____

9. Thinking fifteen to twenty years into the future, what choices need to be made today to reach the future we want for children and for ECE as a professional field of practice?

_____

_____

_____

10. What "drivers" could have the greatest impact in moving ECE forward as a professional field of practice?

_____

_____

_____

Notes

II. Structuring ECE as a Professional Field of Practice

These questions explore the field's defining intent, its distinctive contributions and competence, and the extent to which as a field we are willing to hold ourselves accountable to one another as well as responsible to families and society overall in return for the autonomy to define and govern ECE as a professional field of practice. The questions are further delineated by the three adaptive issues identified in *Ready or Not: Leadership Choices in Early Care and Education*: purpose, identity, and responsibility.[22]

Questions of Purpose

1. What should be ECE's primary purpose as a professional field of practice?

    _____

    _____

    _____

2. To whom should the ECE profession be accountable?

    _____

    _____

    _____

3. What commonalities bind ECE together as a field of practice? How might these commonalities help create a profession with common purpose?

    _____

    _____

    _____

4. What energizes us about the opportunity to form ECE as a professional field of practice?

_____

_____

_____

Questions of Identity

5. What differentiates ECE from other child-serving professions serving the same age children?

_____

_____

_____

6. What are the unique knowledge and skills that should define ECE as a professional field of practice? What makes this expertise distinctive from other child-serving professions?

_____

_____

_____

7. What are strengths and weaknesses of having a variety of entryways for becoming part of ECE?[23]

_____

_____

_____

8. What are strengths of the current menu of ECE degrees, credentials, and in-service and pre-service requirements? What are weaknesses?

_____

_____

_____

9. Where should the bar be set for entry into the profession? What should be the minimum level of preparation expected of the profession's members in terms of education, experience, and examination?

_____

_____

_____

10. In the context of ECE, what does it mean to be an _inclusive_ field of practice?

_____

_____

_____

11. What should be the chronological scope encompassed by ECE? For example:

  a. Children from birth to the start of kindergarten?

  b. Children from birth through kindergarten?

  c. Children from birth through third grade?

  d. Other?

_____

_____

_____

12. Should program setting, ages of children served, and/or sponsors inform expectations for what practitioners need to know and be able to do? If so, in what way?

_____

_____

_____

13. What unifies and what divides ECE as a field of practice across the birth to start of kindergarten age range?[24] Do assumptions about program purpose, program sponsor, or funding stream affect our answers? Should they?

_____

_____

_____

14. What unifies and what divides ECE as a field of practice across the birth to third grade continuum? Do assumptions about program purpose, program sponsor, or funding stream affect our answers? Should they?

_____

_____

_____

15. Who should be "in" the ECE profession, that is, what roles should be included in ECE as a professional field of practice? Some possibilities that have been identified include infant and toddler caregivers, preschool and prekindergarten teachers, kindergarten teachers, primary grade teachers, early intervention specialists, early childhood special education teachers, home visitors, family/home-based child care providers, school-age care/ out-of-school time providers, and nannies.

_____

_____

_____

16. What would be an ideal occupational configuration for ECE as a professional field of practice? For example, are the same obligatory requirements expected of all members regardless of role or does the field have specializations that build on the profession's core knowledge base?

_____

_____

_____

17. What are current occupational strengths that we can build on to move ECE forward as a professional field of practice?

_____

_____

_____

Questions of Responsibility

18. Professions identify to whom they are primarily responsible. To whom is ECE primarily responsible?

_____

_____

_____

19. The bottom line for the medical profession is "do no harm." What should be ECE's bottom line as a professional field of practice?

_____

_____

_____

20. What would have to change to create a shared alternative future for ECE as a professional field of practice?

_____

_____

_____

21. ECE's tough challenge involves adaptive elements. What adaptive challenges will need to be confronted if ECE is to organize as a profession? (Remember: adaptive challenges emerge when responding to conflicting values.)

_____

_____

_____

22. What will we need to learn or change as a field in order to structure ECE as a professional field of practice?

_____

_____

_____

Notes

III. Co-creating ECE as a Professional Field of Practice

These questions anticipate next steps in the field's journey toward becoming a profession and the continued process of coimagining and co-creating ECE's next era.

1. What do we envision as the most important components of the field's change process?

    _____

    _____

    _____

2. What core principals and values should guide the field's decision making about its future?

    _____

    _____

    _____

3. What do we think is the best starting point for structuring ECE as a professional field of practice?

    _____

    _____

    _____

4. What level of agreement should be established to indicate consensus exists for structuring ECE as a profession?

    _____

    _____

    _____

5. Who are constituents or stakeholders who might need to adjust their thinking for ECE to make progress in professionalizing itself as a field of practice?

_____

_____

_____

6. What else do we need to know to engage more fully in the conversations we're having? How might we meet our needs for information and expertise?

_____

_____

_____

7. What one modification could make the most change for ECE as it embarks on structuring itself as a profession?

_____

_____

_____

8. If the world were ideal, what conditions would need to be in place to structure ECE as a profession?

_____

_____

_____

9. What could we change *now* to commence ECE's journey toward professionalizing as a field of practice?

_____

_____

_____

10. What immediate changes can we implement to begin operating from the future we want to create?

_____

_____

_____

11. What questions do we have that lack answers? As a field of practice, are these knowledge gaps serving as obstacles to advancing ECE as a field of practice?

_____

_____

_____

Notes

IV. Questions for Shared Reflection

These questions can be especially meaningful for individual and group reflection and synthesis at the conclusion of conversations with intent.

1. What did you most appreciate about our conversations with intent?

2. What makes you feel most optimistic about ECE's future?

3. What do you see as taking shape? What patterns of thinking are you sensing?

4. Where might we draw inspiration for the systems work that lies ahead?

5. What has been your major learning or insight?

6. What came across from our conversations with intent as new or fresh thinking?

_____

_____

_____

7. What questions were raised for you?

_____

_____

_____

8. Is there a question that if deeply explored could catalyze a breakthrough in our thinking?

_____

_____

_____

9. What energizes you?

_____

_____

_____

10. What commitments are we willing to make—individually or as a group—to move ECE forward as a professional field of practice? What will be the payoff?

_____

_____

_____

Notes

CHAPTER 4

Supporting Successful Conversations
with Intent

THIS BOOK PROVIDES an approach for starting ECE's journey toward becoming a professional field of practice. Now you understand at a deeper level the reasons why ECE needs to confront its tough challenge, restructure its current occupational configuration, and organize as a professional field of practice. You've hopefully considered the questions you need to ask to open yourself to new possibilities (chapter 2). And you're acquainted with the questions the ECE field needs to think through together (chapter 3) so an alternative future for ECE as a field of practice can come to fruition.

Conversations with intent confront our field's fragmented thinking, ripen its readiness to move beyond the status quo, and lay the groundwork for co-creating ECE's next era. By beginning these conversations, the field is launching its first collective action on the way to restructuring ECE as field of practice. As William Isaacs puts it, "New creative action comes only as we expand the bandwidth of what we can accept and what we can seek."[1]

This chapter identifies ways to maximize the interplay of dialogue, skilled discussion, and balanced advocacy. Two of the most important considerations are staying connected to the purpose of conversations with intent and holding true to the unique characteristics of the three conversational forms that provide their backbone. Other considerations are the way in which these conversations are convened, the facilitator's role, and preparing an environment conducive to conversations with intent. Having addressed the first two considerations in previous chapters, this chapter focuses on the last three topics.

The recommendations presented in this chapter are shared as suggestions. They draw from personal experiences as well as recommendations from authors having extensive involvement in designing and facilitating these types of conversations.[2]

Nonetheless, it's expected that your conversations will be customized to your circumstances. Additionally, you'll note the identification of multiple roles. It's presumed these roles can be filled by anyone who is reading this book.

This is exciting and important work. It represents a milestone in ECE's evolution as a field. If you're interested in learning with and from others also engaged with re-thinking ECE as a field of practice, contact eceleadership@gmail.com, and I'll share the link to "ECE Pioneers for the New Era," which is an online community. What you've learned, you're currently pondering, and you're presently doing related to the five overarching questions that frame conversations with intent is at the heart of our community. (See Overarching Questions Framing Conversations with Intent.)

CONVENING CONVERSATIONS WITH INTENT

Conversations with intent can be convened at the community, state, regional, and national levels. Their hosts can be individuals, organizations, or associations. Group size can also vary, though a minimum of ten to twelve participants is typically recommended for conversations grounded in dialogue. If your intent is to lift up differences among the field's subgroups, a minimum group size of twenty increases the range of views available. If a larger group is coming together, perhaps because convened as part of a local, state, regional, or national conference, you might want to consider using the World Café or a Café-style approach. Drawing on seven design principles consistent with conversations with intent, the World Café methodology provides an organized format for hosting large group dialogue that fosters people's collective ability to share knowledge and build common meaning. Its flexibility permits it to be used with groups of various sizes.[3]

The design of conversations with intent should reflect their purpose. Assuming you're not hosting a conference session, this starts with the invitation list. Participants need not know each other in advance of the conversation, but they do need to know the conversation's intent:

> **OVERARCHING QUESTIONS FRAMING CONVERSATIONS WITH INTENT**
>
> 1. What major choices will be required to move ECE forward as a profession? Are we prepared as a field of practice to make them?
>
> 2. What principles or values should guide formation of ECE as a professional field of practice?
>
> 3. What options are available for ECE's organization as a professional field of practice?
>
> 4. What should be the starting place(s) for structuring ECE as a profession?
>
> 5. What else do we need to know to move forward? Who else should we be learning from?

- coming together as a field of practice to move beyond the limits of our individual understanding;

- coimagining different possibilities for organizing ECE as a professional field of practice; and

- laying the groundwork for formally structuring ECE as a profession.

This means diverse viewpoints have to be present so conversations with intent can function as "incubators for new thinking."[4]

Invitees ideally will have read at least the first two chapters of this book. This knowledge will help ensure awareness of the field's tough challenge and what "the next era" is about. They should be encouraged to reflect on the questions presented in chapter 2 of this guide so they arrive more aware of their mental models and prepared to enter into conversations with intent as listeners and cothinkers.

Conversations with intent ask participants to think with each other in new ways. Plan at least for an hour and a half to a two-hour conversation. Giving participants the opportunity to more deeply inquire into issues by engaging in multiple conversations can be especially worthwhile.

As a way to initiate a new collaborative relationship and create shared ownership of the convening, consider having hosts with different roles in the field arrange the meeting, such as teachers, administrators, resource and referral providers, professional development providers, and higher education faculty. Or create a similarly diverse small subgroup of invitees to review the questions in chapter 3 and prepare an assortment for the larger group's selection once together on-site. If the conversational group is not too large, invitees could potentially identify questions they find of most interest in advance of conversations with intent via an electronic survey.

While planning for these conversations should be driven by intentionality, creating an informal atmosphere helps people feel more comfortable. It's hard to anticipate in advance of conversations with intent how the interactions will flow or to know the questions participants will find most engaging. Consequently, preparing a topical vs. tightly controlled agenda is recommended.

This doesn't mean the time together should be a free-for-all, however. Although a facilitator wants to be in a position "to go with the flow," it's also important for the conversation to stay on track. The length of time for exploring each question can vary, depending on the question's complexity. As a general guideline, twenty to thirty minutes should be allowed for each question so that sufficient time is available for reflecting upon and inquiring into the assumptions and viewpoints in the room. Remember: These conversations aren't intended to resolve our different ways of thinking or convince others to change what they think. Instead, they're meant to expand our shared understanding of ECE's tough challenge, jointly imagine options for restructuring ECE as a field of practice, and lay the foundation for next phases of the field's journey toward professionalism.

THE FACILITATOR'S ROLE

The conversation's facilitator should be someone who understands the purpose of conversations with intent, how they differ from usual ways of conversing with one another, and the distinctions among the conversational forms being used to foster reflection, mutual exploration, and expanded understanding of ECE as a field of practice. The facilitator is not there to steer the conversation in a particular direction. Rather his or her role is to set the context—keeping the focus on the conversation's purpose and ensuring the conversational space to explore different views and possibilities is maintained.

> **THE ESSENCE OF CONVERSATIONS WITH INTENT**
> - Contribute your thinking and experience.
> - Listen to understand.
> - Connect ideas.
> - Listen together for patterns, insights, and deeper questions.[1]

When setting the stage for the conversations, the facilitator will want to review the conversation's purpose; highlight the essence of these conversations (see The Essence of Conversations with Intent); and remind participants of the three foundational practices of conversations with intent: *listening*, *respecting*, and *suspending* (see chapter 3, pages 33–34). Since thinking together is a high priority and we in ECE are avid advocates, it might be worth reminding participants they're not present to engage others with their personal agenda.

Encouraging people to "speak to the center" rather than to each other individually or to the facilitator is another way to reinforce conversations with intent as a "conversation of the whole."[5]

When the conversation is in need of an assist so the inquiry or skilled discussion can move forward, there are three ways to respond. First, the facilitator can draw on suggestions about getting up on the balcony (chapter 3, page 34); second, she or he can note what seems to be emerging as interactions connect and weave together (sensor role); or third, she or he can serve in the roles of bystander or clarifier (see Conversational Roles, chapter 3, page 35). The facilitator can also invite the group to step up and perform one of these functions. For example: "Is there anyone who's stepped up on the balcony who can help us see the bigger picture of what's going on?" As much as possible, the facilitator should encourage group participants to be engaged with one another and assume responsibility for the conversation's deepening inquiry into ECE as a field of practice.

> A facilitator needs to be viewed as neutral.

A facilitator needs to be viewed as neutral. A neutral stance may be harder to achieve, though, if the facilitator is seen within the ECE community as having a strong point of view about the field or about a contentious issue. This doesn't mean the facilitator lacks a point of view on issues, but during conversations with intent, the facilitator has to be seen as embodying the conversation's principles and intentions and not be seen as the "leader" or as leading the conversation. In conversations with intent, each of us is being asked to step forward to exercise leadership on behalf of an alternative future for ECE.

This means the individual preparation outlined in chapter 2 is as important for facilitators as it is for invitees. They'll want to be conscious of their personal triggers. They also should be capable of embracing polarized views so a conversation can move into inquiry about differences that may be raising the temperature in the room. Examples of questions that help navigate these moments include "What questions might we ask to deepen our understanding of the differences in viewpoint being expressed?" or "What is the ground *between* the views being expressed?"[6] Another possible intervention is "The way we are talking now—each one advocating, no one inquiring, everyone defending positions—repeats exchanges (we've had). Do people see this? Can we make an effort to do something else?" or "What might we learn that's new from each other?" or "Why do each of us feel pressured to defend ourselves?"[7] Additional questions for deepening inquiry and maintaining shared focus on the conversation's collective intent are available under Questions to Facilitate Meaningful Dialogue (see chapter 3, pages 38–39).

PREPARING THE LEARNING ENVIRONMENT

The learning environment matters for conversations with intent. We're being asked to explore questions that have personal meaning and tap into deeply held beliefs. Proposals that potentially create an alternative future for ECE could do the same for some of us personally. This is the rationale for the suggestion offered in chapter 3 to imagine ECE is being built from scratch following a tsunami and to identify a date in the future for the work's completion. A sense of safety and trust in the process is necessary so participants will be forthcoming in sharing their mental models, able to moderate their defensiveness, and open to inquiring about others' assumptions.

Attending to the Conversational Setting

While we're not always comfortable admitting it, mistrust, competition, and sometimes even disrespect dwell within ECE in regard to programs from different sectors, between the for-profit and nonprofit parts of our field, and between community and school-based programs, among other divisions that coexist within our field. While these feelings rarely are expressed publicly, they are part of ECE's fabric, which underscores the importance of hosting conversations in spaces perceived by all participants as neutral. This consideration adds value to invitations that come from cohosts with different roles and "living" in different sectors of the field, thereby conveying the intent to explore ECE from the perspective of the whole, not just some of its parts.

Ways to "warm" the space will vary depending on whether you're in someone's home, an office space, or attending a conference. Designating a few invitees to greet other guests as they enter the room conveys a personally welcoming tone that helps distinguish the gathering from other exchanges. Pictures of children propped on easels or taped to a wall remind us that these conversations are about something larger than our individual roles or ambitions—that we've gathered together for the purpose of learning with and from each other to rethink ECE's present occupational configuration so it can evolve toward becoming a professional field of practice.

Other possibilities could include homey touches such as art, greenery, or children's toys. Early educators know the learning environment matters. We simply need to bring this sensitivity to bear when hosting conversations with intent.

If the group is twelve or fewer individuals, arrange chairs in a circle so participants face one another. This conversational arrangement fosters more intimate interaction than is created when sitting around a board table, for instance. If the group's size exceeds twelve individuals, try seating participants around round tables, with no more than four to five individuals at each table. The World Café is noted for covering its tables with white paper "tablecloths" so participants can doodle, record thoughts, and so forth during a conversation.

Limiting table conversations to four to five people makes it easier for everyone to participate and extends the time available for deeper exploration of different assumptions. Think how different meal conversations are when guests are lined up along the sides of a dining table. Instead of participating in a whole group conversation, people sitting next to or across from each other tend to engage only with one another. The key take away here is the importance of creating an inclusive sense of community among people coming together to engage in mutual learning and exploration.

Reminding invitees as part of their invitation or in a follow-up reminder to review the Keep in Minds (chapter 3, pages 36–38) prior to the convening can be helpful. They were shared for the purpose of enlarging individual and collective ability to expand and enrich these conversations.

Opening and Closing the Conversation

GETTING STARTED. Allowing time for participants to mingle before starting the conversation brings energy into the room and helps people get to know one another. Greeters, if present, are encouraged to initiate introductions between people who may not know one another. When accompanied by comments such as "Person X has such good ideas," or "Person Y is such a creative thinker," participants know from the outset that their contributions are being viewed as important to the conversation. If a large group is assembled, hosts can visit individual tables, introducing themselves and learning who is present in the room; this helps reduce the sense of anonymity.

Depending on the group's size, "checking in" at the beginning of the conversation to give each participant an opportunity to speak for a minute about what they're thinking or feeling or have noticed helps create an immediate sense of community

REMINDERS FOR HOSTS AND FACILITATORS

1. Stay connected to the purpose of conversations with intent (see chapter 1).

2. Hold true to the distinctive characteristics of dialogue, skilled discussion, and balanced advocacy.

3. Remind conversation participants to place their thinking in the context of the five overarching questions (see Overarching Questions Framing Conversations with Intent).

4. Invite individuals representing ECE's diverse sectors and roles and who offer varied viewpoints about ECE as a field of practice.

5. Encourage invitees to become familiar with this guide or other writing about the need to restructure ECE as a field of practice.

6. Encourage invitees to come prepared for the conversation by reflecting on their mental models about ECE as a field of practice (see chapter 2).

7. Create an inviting and informal conversational learning environment.

8. Reiterate or post the essence of conversations with intent (see The Essence of Conversations with Intent).

9. Encourage participants to use the three practices essential to effective conversations: listening, respecting, and suspending.

10. Allow sufficient time for exploring individual questions, yet be comfortable with allowing the inquiry to remain unresolved in terms of reaching consensus on issues being examined.

and sends the message that everyone will have air time.[8] If warranted by the group size or lack of familiarity among participants, a poster taped to the wall can encourage participants to introduce themselves to one another at their individual tables using questions such as "What do we need to know about one another so we can engage together in a conversation about ECE's future as a professional field of practice?"

BRINGING CLOSURE. Giving consideration to the conversation's closure is as important as attending to the conversation's start. If additional conversations or other next steps are planned, this is a good time to share them. If you want to encourage participants to stay in touch with one another, offer the means for doing so. Questions for Shared Reflections at the conclusion of chapter 3 (pages 57–58) offer possibilities for bringing closure and also signal that these conversations will have a life beyond the time just spent together.

If time is available for sharing information from multiple small groups, Juanita Brown suggests rethinking this routine technique and reimagining it as a "conversation of the whole."[9] This is achieved by asking participants to share their responses in a way that contribute to a "knowledge web" by weaving together thoughts as they are being expressed—what a poetic phrase for describing the aim of this book.

Each of us should accept responsibility not only for participating in conversations with intent but also for convening them. And don't forget: if you or your conversation participants are interested in learning with and from others engaged with rethinking ECE as a field of practice, contact eceleadership@gmail.com, and I'll share the link to the online community "ECE Pioneers for the New Era." What you have learned, are currently pondering, and/or are presently doing related to the five overarching questions that frame conversations with intent is at the heart of our community. "ECE Pioneers for the New Era" is our route to moving beyond individual conversational gatherings and generating a field-wide conversation so a true "conversation of the whole" is created. A summary of these suggestions for hosts and facilitators can be found in Reminders for Hosts and Facilitators.

GUIDING ECE INTO ITS NEXT ERA

In my previous book, *Early Childhood Education for a New Era: Leading for Our Profession*, I suggested ECE was in the midst of a defining moment and that as a field of practice, we were in a developmental phase identified as "Systems Building and Self-Realization." This book is written in hopes the ECE field will structure itself with interconnected and interdependent systems of preparation, practice, and accountability bound together by shared purpose. By structuring itself as a professional field of practice, ECE can realize its potential and fulfill its promise to children, families, and to society.

This aspiration, though, depends on each of us—individually and collectively—becoming engaged with redirecting ECE's trajectory. The alternative, of course, is to continue accommodating the status quo and marginalizing ECE's impact as a field of practice. *Professionalizing Early Childhood Education As a Field of Practice: A Guide to the Next Era* was written to spark the dialogue, discussion, and ultimately the decision-making and action that can create a more deserving future for ECE as a field of practice.

REMINDERS: CONTINUED

11. Foster reflection, mutual exploration, and expanded understanding of ECE as a field of practice. As facilitator, set the context, keep the focus on the conversation's purpose, and ensure "conversational space" is available to explore different assumptions and possibilities. Maintain a neutral stance, being careful not to steer the conversation in a particular direction.

12. Try to create a "conversation of the whole."

13. Conclude the conversation with questions that help participants reflect upon and synthesize their experience (see Questions for Shared Reflection, chapter 3).

14. To signal that these conversations have a life beyond the time just spent together, share how everyone can become part of "ECE Pioneers for a New Era" by e-mailing eceleadership@gmail.com.

15. Encourage participants to convene their own conversations with intent so participation in these conversations continually increases and becomes more inclusive of the field's diverse viewpoints.

> By becoming a profession, ECE can realize its potential and fulfill its promise to children, families, and to society.

Endnotes

Acknowledgments

1. National Association for the Education of Young Children, *Strategic Direction.*

Chapter 1

1. Goffin, *Early Childhood Education for a New Era: Leading for Our Profession*, xviii. The name for ECE goes to the heart of our identity issue as a field of practice. I have chosen *early childhood education* because it succinctly states what I believe to be the field's purpose and encompasses its multiple sectors and commitments to early learning, responsive and caring relationships, and early development.

2. Conklin, "Wicked Problems and Social Complexity."

3. A more detailed diagnosis and rationale for professionalizing ECE can be found in *Ready or Not: Leadership Choices in Early Care and Education* and *Early Childhood Education for a New Era: Leading for Our Profession*, both by the author.

4. Goffin, *Early Childhood Education for a New Era: Leading for Our Profession*, 8.

5. Barnett, "Effectiveness of Early Educational Interventions;" Early et al, *Pre-Kindergarten in Eleven States: NCEDL's Multi-State Study of Pre-Kindergarten & Study of State-Wide Early Education Programs (SWEEP)*; Shonkoff, "Protecting Brains, Not Simply Stimulating Minds." Additionally, in December 2014 over seven hundred researchers signed an "ECE Consensus Letter for Researchers," highlighting the widespread agreement among researchers about the value of investments in quality early childhood education programs (http://nieer.org/publications/ece-consensus-letter-researchers).

6. Barnett, "Effectiveness of Early Educational Interventions."

7. Goffin, *Early Childhood Education for a New Era: Leading for Our Profession.*

8. Meadows, *Thinking in Systems: A Primer*; Senge, Hamilton, and Kania, "The Dawn of System Leadership."

9. Kagan and Cohen, *Reinventing Early Care and Education: A Vision for a Quality System*; Kagan and Cohen, *Not by Chance: Creating an Early Care and Education System for America's Children*.

10. Goffin, "Beyond Systemic Structures: Penetrating to the Core of an Early Care and Education System;" Goffin, *Early Childhood Education for a New Era: Leading for Our Profession*.

11. Goffin, *Field-Wide Leadership: Insights from Five Fields of Practice*; Dower, O'Neil, and Hough, *Profiling the Professions: A Model for Evaluating Emerging Health Professions*.

12. Heifetz, *Leadership without Easy Answers*; Isaacs, *Dialogue and the Art of Thinking Together: A Pioneering Approach to Communicating in Business and in Life*; Senge et al, *The Necessary Revolution: How Individuals and Organizations Are Working Together to Create a Sustainable World*; Senge, Hamilton, and Kania, "The Dawn of System Leadership."

13. Jaworski, *Synchronicity: The Inner Path of Leadership*; Kurtzman, *Common Purpose: How Great Leaders Get Organizations to Achieve the Extraordinary*; Ready and Truelove, "The Power of Collective Ambition;" Senge, *The Fifth Discipline: The Art and Practice of the Learning Organization*; Senge et al, *Presence: An Exploration of Profound Change in People, Organizations, and Society*.

14. Dower, O'Neil, and Hough, *Profiling the Professions: A Model for Evaluating Emerging Health Professions*, 5.

15. Senge, *The Fifth Discipline: The Art and Practice of the Learning Organization*, 9.

16. Starr, *The Social Transformation of American Medicine: The Rise of a Sovereign Profession and the Making of a Vast Industry*; Woods, *From Craft to Profession: The Practice of Architecture in Nineteenth-Century America*; Brandon and Welch, *The History of Financial Planning: The Transformation of Financial Services*; Flanagan, *One Strong Voice: The Story of the American Nurses' Association*; Schumann, foreword in *Early Childhood Education for a New Era: Leading for Our Profession*; Goldstein and Beebe, "National Association of Social Workers;" National Council of Architectural Registration Boards, *The History of NCARB*.

17. Senge et al, *The Necessary Revolution: How Individuals and Organizations Are Working Together to Create a Sustainable World*, 141.

18. Heifetz, Grashow, and Linsky, *The Practice of Adaptive Leadership: Tools and Tactics for Changing Your Organization and the World*; Kahane, *Transformative Scenario Planning: Working Together to Change the Future*; Senge et al, *The Fifth Discipline Fieldbook: Strategies and Tools for Building a Learning Organization*; Senge, Hamilton, and Kania, "The Dawn of System Leadership."

19. Kahane, *Power and Love: A Theory and Practice of Social Change*.

20. Kahane, *Power and Love: A Theory and Practice of Social Change*, 5.

21. Heifetz, Grashow, and Linsky, *The Practice of Adaptive Leadership: Tools and Tactics for Changing Your Organization and the World*; Linsky and Heifetz, foreword in *Ready or Not: Leadership Choices in Early Care and Education*.

22. Linsky and Heifetz, foreword in *Ready or Not: Leadership Choices in Early Care and Education*.

23. Senge, Hamilton, and Kania, "The Dawn of System Leadership;" Meadows, *Thinking in Systems: A Primer*.

24. Heifetz, Grashow, and Linsky, *The Practice of Adaptive Leadership: Tools and Tactics for Changing Your Organization and the World*; Isaacs, *Dialogue and the Art of Thinking Together: A Pioneering Approach to Communicating in Business and in Life*; Jaworski, *Synchronicity: The Inner Path of Leadership*; Kahane, *Transformative Scenario Planning: Working Together to Change the Future*; Senge et al, *The Necessary Revolution: How Individuals and Organizations Are Working Together to Create a Sustainable World*; Senge, Hamilton, and Kania, "The Dawn of System Leadership."

25. Heifetz, *Leadership without Easy Answers*; Kahane, *Power and Love: A Theory and Practice of Social Change*.

26. Brown, *The World Café: Shaping Our Futures through Conversations That Matter*; Isaacs, *Dialogue and the Art of Thinking Together: A Pioneering Approach to Communicating in Business and in Life*; Ross, "Skillful Discussion: Protocols for Reaching a Decision—Mindfully."

27. Brown, *The World Café: Shaping Our Futures through Conversations That Matter*, 19 (italics in original).

28. Ross, "Skillful Discussion: Protocols for Reaching a Decision—Mindfully;" Isaacs, *Dialogue and the Art of Thinking Together: A Pioneering Approach to Communicating in Business and in Life*.

29. Kegan and Lahey, *Immunity to Change: How to Overcome It and Unlock Potential in Yourself and Your Organization*, 11.

30. Heifetz, *Leadership without Easy Answers*; Kahane, *Power and Love: A Theory and Practice of Social Change*; Senge, Hamilton, and Kania, "The Dawn of System Leadership;" Senge et al, *The Necessary Revolution: How Individuals and Organizations Are Working Together to Create a Sustainable World*.

31. Kahane, *Transformative Scenario Planning: Working Together to Change the Future*.

32. Senge, Hamilton, and Kania, "The Dawn of System Leadership."

33. Senge, *The Fifth Discipline: The Art and Practice of the Learning Organization*, 8.

34. Senge, Hamilton, and Kania, "The Dawn of System Leadership."

35. Isaacs, *Dialogue and the Art of Thinking Together: A Pioneering Approach to Communicating in Business and in Life*; Ross, "Skillful Discussion: Protocols for Reaching a Decision—Mindfully."

36. Meadows, *Thinking in Systems: A Primer*.

37. Meadows, *Thinking in Systems: A Primer*.

38. Goffin and Washington, *Ready or Not: Leadership Choices in Early Care and Education*.

39. Meadows, *Thinking in Systems: A Primer*, 7.

40. Meadows, *Thinking in Systems: A Primer*.

41. White and Buka, "Early Education: Programs, Traditions, and Policies."

42. Spodek and Walberg, introduction in *Early Childhood Education: Issues and Insights*.

43. Goffin, *Early Childhood Education for a New Era: Leading for Our Profession*. See Appendix.

44. Goffin, *Early Childhood Education for a New Era: Leading for Our Profession*.

45. Kegan and Lahey, *How the Way We Talk Can Change the Way We Work: Seven Languages for Transformation*.

46. Heifetz, *Leadership without Easy Answers*.

47. Goffin, *Early Childhood Education for a New Era: Leading for Our Profession*.

48. Goffin, *Early Childhood Education for a New Era: Leading for Our Profession*. See chapter 3 for a compilation of the field's documented concerns.

49. Heifetz, *Leadership without Easy Answers*.

50. *The Fifth Discipline Fieldbook* by Senge and his colleagues, published in 1994, builds on Senge's 1990 classic, *The Fifth Discipline*. It is accessible and includes concrete guidance and suggested language related to dialogue, inquiry, skilled discussion, and balancing advocacy and inquiry, among other topics. William Isaacs's *Dialogue and the Art of Thinking Together* is oriented to the conceptual and theoretical basis of dialogue, but also offers how-to information. Juanita Brown's book on the World Café provides a clear rationale for the value of conversations as change levers, offers specifics on hosting World Cafés, and presents numerous examples of its use written by those who have used this approach to advance their work.

51. Heifetz, *Leadership without Easy Answers*.

Definitions Sidebar Notes

1. Wheatley, *Leadership and the New Science: Discovering Order in a Chaotic World*.

2. Goffin, *Early Childhood Education for a New Era: Leading for Our Profession*.

3. Goffin, *Early Childhood Education for a New Era: Leading for Our Profession*.

4. Meadows, *Thinking in Systems: A Primer*, 2.

5. Senge, *The Fifth Discipline: The Art and Practice of the Learning Organization*, 8.

Chapter 2

1. Meadows, *Thinking in Systems: A Primer*, 4 (italics in original).

2. Fullan, *Choosing the Wrong Drivers for Whole System Reform*, 5.

3. Goffin, *Early Childhood Education for a New Era: Leading for Our Profession*.

4. Roberts, "What You Can Expect . . . in Working with Mental Models."

5. Kahane, *Transformative Scenario Planning: Working Together to Change the Future*, xv.

6. Kegan and Lahey, *Immunity to Change: How to Overcome It and Unlock Potential in Yourself and Your Organization*, 18.

7. Kegan and Lahey, *Immunity to Change: How to Overcome It and Unlock Potential in Yourself and Your Organization*, 51.

8. Kegan and Lahey, *How the Way We Talk Can Change the Way We Work: Seven Languages for Transformation*, 68 (italics in original).

9. Kegan and Lahey, *How the Way We Talk Can Change the Way We Work: Seven Languages for Transformation*, 86.

10. Jaworski, *Synchronicity: The Inner Path of Leadership*; Senge et al, *The Fifth Discipline Fieldbook: Strategies and Tools for Building a Learning Organization*.

11. Roberts, "What You Can Expect . . . in Working with Mental Models;" Heifetz, Grashow, and Linsky, *The Practice of Adaptive Leadership: Tools and Tactics for Changing Your Organization and the World*.

12. Brown, *The World Café: Shaping Our Futures through Conversations That Matter*; Goffin and Washington, *Ready or Not: Leadership Choices in Early Care and Education*; Heifetz, Grashow, and Linsky, *The Practice of Adaptive Leadership: Tools and Tactics for Changing Your Organization and the World*; Homer, "Conflicted Café? How to Deal with Differences and Tension;" Isaacs, *Dialogue and the Art of Thinking Together: A Pioneering Approach to Communicating in Business and in Life*; Isaacs, "Accessing Genuine Dialogue;" Isaacs and Smith, "General Guidelines for Dialogue Sessions;" Kansas Leadership Center, *Civic Leadership Play Book*; Kegan and Lahey, *Immunity to Change: How to Overcome It and Unlock Potential in Yourself and Your Organization*; Senge et al, *The Fifth Discipline*

Fieldbook: Strategies and Tools for Building a Learning Organization; Ross, "Skillful Discussion: Protocols for Reaching a Decision—Mindfully;" Stanfield, *The Art of Focused Conversation: 100 Ways to Access Group Wisdom in the Workplace.*

13. Zander and Zander, *The Art of Possibility: Transforming Professional and Personal Life.*

Chapter 3

1. Fritz, *Path of Least Resistance: Learning to Become the Creative Force in Your Own Life,* 11 (italics in original).

2. Brown, *The World Café: Shaping Our Futures through Conversations That Matter;* Isaacs, *Dialogue and the Art of Thinking Together: A Pioneering Approach to Communicating in Business and in Life;* Senge et al, *Presence: An Exploration of Profound Change in People, Organizations, and Society.*

3. Isaacs, *Dialogue and the Art of Thinking Together: A Pioneering Approach to Communicating in Business and in Life,* 335.

4. Brown, *The World Café: Shaping Our Futures through Conversations That Matter;* Cooperrider and Whitney, *Appreciative Inquiry: A Positive Revolution in Change;* Vogt, Brown, and Isaacs, *The Art of Powerful Questions: Catalyzing Insight, Innovation, and Action.*

5. Isaacs, *Dialogue and the Art of Thinking Together: A Pioneering Approach to Communicating in Business and in Life;* Senge et al, *The Fifth Discipline Fieldbook: Strategies and Tools for Building a Learning Organization;* Senge et al, *Presence: An Exploration of Profound Change in People, Organizations, and Society.*

6. Ross and Roberts, "Balancing Inquiry and Advocacy."

7. Heifetz, Grashow, and Linsky, *The Practice of Adaptive Leadership: Tools and Tactics for Changing Your Organization and the World.*

8. Fritz, *Path of Least Resistance: Learning to Become the Creative Force in Your Own Life;* Senge et al, *The Fifth Discipline Fieldbook: Strategies and Tools for Building a Learning Organization;* Kegan and Lahey, *Immunity to Change: How to Overcome It and Unlock Potential in Yourself and Your Organization;* Heifetz, Grashow, and Linsky, *The Practice of Adaptive Leadership: Tools and Tactics for Changing Your*

Organization and the World; Isaacs, *Dialogue and the Art of Thinking Together: A Pioneering Approach to Communicating in Business and in Life;* Senge et al, *The Necessary Revolution: How Individuals and Organizations Are Working Together to Create a Sustainable World;* Stone, Patton, and Heen, *Difficult Conversations: How to Discuss What Matters Most.*

9. Heifetz, Grashow, and Linsky, *The Practice of Adaptive Leadership: Tools and Tactics for Changing Your Organization and the World.*

10. Kegan and Lahey, *Immunity to Change: How to Overcome It and Unlock Potential in Yourself and Your Organization,* 54.

11. My appreciation to Tracy Benson of the Waters Foundation for this suggestion.

12. Standfield, *The Art of Focused Conversation: 100 Ways to Access Group Wisdom in the Workplace;* Vogt, Brown, and Isaacs, *The Art of Powerful Questions: Catalyzing Insight, Innovation, and Action.*

13. Heifetz, Grashow, and Linsky, *The Practice of Adaptive Leadership: Tools and Tactics for Changing Your Organization and the World.*

14. Goodlad, "The Occupation of Teaching in Schools," 29.

15. Senge, afterword in *The World Café: Shaping Our Futures through Conversations That Matter,* 219.

16. Senge, afterword in *The World Café: Shaping Our Futures through Conversations That Matter,* 220.

17. Brown, *The World Café: Shaping Our Futures through Conversations That Matter;* Goffin and Washington, *Ready or Not: Leadership Choices in Early Care and Education;* Heifetz, Grashow, and Linsky, *The Practice of Adaptive Leadership: Tools and Tactics for Changing Your Organization and the World;* Homer, "Conflicted Café? How to Deal with Differences and Tension;" Isaacs, *Dialogue and the Art of Thinking Together: A Pioneering Approach to Communicating in Business and in Life;* Isaacs, "Accessing Genuine Dialogue;" Isaacs and Smith, "General Guidelines for Dialogue Sessions;" Kansas Leadership Center, *Civic Leadership Play Book;* Kegan and Lahey, *Immunity to Change: How to Overcome It and Unlock Potential in Yourself and Your Organization;* Senge et al, *The Fifth Discipline*

Fieldbook: Strategies and Tools for Building a Learning Organization; Ross, "Skillful Discussion: Protocols for Reaching a Decision—Mindfully;" Stanfield, *The Art of Focused Conversation: 100 Ways to Access Group Wisdom in the Workplace.*

18. Vogt, Brown, and Isaacs, *The Art of Powerful Questions: Catalyzing Insight, Innovation, and Action.*

19. My appreciation to Mary Jean Schumann, author of the foreword to *Early Childhood Education for a New Era: Leading for Our Profession,* for this suggestion.

20. Senge et al, *The Necessary Revolution: How Individuals and Organizations Are Working Together to Create a Sustainable World,* 141. As presented, the original quote's pronouns have been changed so personalized to those of us engaged in the quest to structure ECE as a professional field of practice.

21. Thank you to Jim Squires for suggesting this question.

22. Goffin and Washington, *Ready or Not: Leadership Choices in Early Care and Education.*

23. Thank you to Deb Flis for suggesting this and the next question.

24. This question and the variation in the question that follows is based on an exploration that took place during the National Association of Early Childhood Specialists in State Departments of Education's (NAECS_SDE) 2014 Annual Meeting.

Conversational Roles Sidebar Note

1. Adapted from Ross and Roberts, "Balancing Inquiry and Advocacy," 254.

Characteristics of Professional Fields of Practice Sidebar Notes

1. Goffin, *Early Childhood Education for a New Era: Leading for Our Profession.*

2. Goffin, *Early Childhood Education for a New Era: Leading for Our Profession.*

Chapter 4

1. Isaacs, "Accessing Genuine Dialogue," 11.

2. Brown, *The World Café: Shaping Our Futures through Conversations That Matter;* Isaacs, *Dialogue and the Art of Thinking Together: A Pioneering Approach to Communicating in Business and in Life;* Senge et al, *The Fifth Discipline Fieldbook: Strategies and Tools for Building a Learning Organization;* Isaacs and Smith, "General Guidelines for Dialogue Sessions;" Stanfield, *The Art of Focused Conversation: 100 Ways to Access Group Wisdom in the Workplace.*

3. Brown, *The World Café: Shaping Our Futures through Conversations That Matter,* 67.

4. Brown, *The World Café: Shaping Our Futures through Conversations That Matter.* World Café resources can also be found at www.theworldcafe.org.

5. Brown, *The World Café: Shaping Our Futures through Conversations That Matter;* Isaacs, *Dialogue and the Art of Thinking Together: A Pioneering Approach to Communicating in Business and in Life;* Isaacs and Smith, "General Guidelines for Dialogue Sessions." "Speaking to the center" underlines creation of a pool of common meaning and moderates interpersonal dynamics.

6. Isaacs, *Dialogue and the Art of Thinking Together: A Pioneering Approach to Communicating in Business and in Life,* 376.

7. Isaacs, *Dialogue and the Art of Thinking Together: A Pioneering Approach to Communicating in Business and in Life,* 368.

8. Isaacs and Smith, "General Guidelines for Dialogue Sessions."

9. Brown, *The World Café: Shaping Our Futures through Conversations That Matter,* 65.

The Essence of Conversations with Intent Sidebar Notes

1. Brown, *The World Café: Shaping Our Futures through Conversations That Matter,* 167. In the context of the World Café, Brown identified these habits as etiquette principles.

References

Barnett, W. Steven. "Effectiveness of Early Educational Interventions." *Science* 333, no. 6045 (2011): 975–78.

Brandon Jr., E. Denby, and H. Oliver Welch. *The History of Financial Planning: The Transformation of Financial Services*. Hoboken, NJ: John Wiley, 2009.

Brown, Juanita, ed. *The World Café: Shaping Our Futures through Conversations That Matter*. San Francisco: Berrett-Koehler, 2005.

Conklin, Jeffrey. "Wicked Problems and Social Complexity." In *Dialogue Mapping: Building Shared Understanding of Wicked Problems*, 3–40. Hoboken, NJ: John Wiley, 2006. http://cognexus.org/wpf/wickedproblems.pdf.

Cooperrider, David L., and Diana Whitney. *Appreciative Inquiry: A Positive Revolution in Change*. San Francisco: Berrett-Koehler, 2005.

Dower, Catherine, Edward H. O'Neil, and Holly J. Hough. *Profiling the Professions: A Model for Evaluating Emerging Health Professions*. San Francisco: Center for the Health Professions, University of California, 2001. https://nasemso.org /EMSEducationImplementationPlanning/documents/Model2.pdf.

Early, Diane M. et al. *Pre-Kindergarten in Eleven States: NCEDL's Multi-State Study of Pre-Kindergarten & Study of State-Wide Early Education Programs (SWEEP)*. Preliminary descriptive report. Chapel Hill: University of North Carolina, 2005. http://fpg.unc.edu/sites/fpg.unc.edu /files/resources/reports-and-policy-briefs/NCEDL_PreK-in-Eleven-States_Working -Paper_2005.pdf.

Flanagan, Lyndia. *One Strong Voice: The Story of the American Nurses' Association*. Kansas City, MO: The American Nurses Association, 1976.

Fritz, Robert. *Path of Least Resistance: Learning to Become the Creative Force in Your Own Life*. New York: Fawcett Columbine, 1989.

Fullan, Michael. *Choosing the Wrong Drivers for Whole System Reform*. Seminar Series paper no. 204. East Melbourne, Australia: Centre for Strategic Education, 2011. http://edsource.org/wp-content/uploads/Fullan-Wrong-Drivers1.pdf

Goffin, Stacie G. *Field-Wide Leadership: Insights from Five Fields of Practice*. Washington, DC: Goffin Strategy Group, 2009. www.goffinstrategygroup.com.

———. "Beyond Systemic Structures: Penetrating to the Core of an Early Care and Education System." In *Early Childhood Systems: Transforming Early Learning*, edited by Sharon L. Kagan and Kristie Kauerz, 267–82. New York: Teachers College Press, 2012.

———. *Early Childhood Education for a New Era: Leading for Our Profession*. New York: Teachers College Press, 2013.

Goffin, Stacie G., and Valora Washington. *Ready or Not: Leadership Choices in Early Care and Education*. New York: Teachers College Press, 2007.

Goldstein, Sheldon R., and Linda Beebe. "National Association of Social Workers." In *Encyclopedia of Social Work, 19th edition*, edited by Richard L. Edwards, 1747–64. Washington, DC: NASW Press, 1994.

Goodlad, John I. "The Occupation of Teaching in Schools." In *The Moral Dimensions of Teaching*, edited by John I. Goodlad, Roger Soder, and Kenneth A. Sirotnik, 3–34. San Francisco: Jossey-Bass, 1990.

Heifetz, Ronald A. *Leadership without Easy Answers*. Cambridge, MA: Belknap Press, 1994.

Heifetz, Ronald, Alexander Grashow, and Marty Linsky. *The Practice of Adaptive Leadership: Tools and Tactics for Changing Your Organization and the World*. Boston: Harvard Business Press, 2009.

Homer, Ken. "Conflicted Café? How to Deal with Differences and Tension." In *The World Café: Shaping Our Futures through Conversations That Matter*, edited by Juanita Brown, 169–75. San Francisco: Berrett-Koehler, 2005.

Isaacs, William. *Dialogue and the Art of Thinking Together: A Pioneering Approach to Communicating in Business and in Life*. New York: Currency, 1999.

———. "Accessing Genuine Dialogue." *The Watercooler*, blog, 2012. http://watercoolernewsletter.com/accessing-genuine-dialogue#.VQUSabPF8qa.

Isaacs, William, and Bryan Smith. "General Guidelines for Dialogue Sessions." In *The Fifth Discipline Fieldbook: Strategies and Tools for Building a Learning Organization*, edited by Peter M. Senge, Art Kleiner, Charlotte Roberts, Richard B. Ross, and Bryan J. Smith, 379–80. New York: Currency, 1994.

Jaworski, Joseph. *Synchronicity: The Inner Path of Leadership*. San Francisco: Berrett-Koehler, 2011.

Kagan, Sharon L., and Nancy E. Cohen, eds. *Reinventing Early Care and Education: A Vision for a Quality System*. San Francisco: Jossey-Bass, 1996.

———. *Not by Chance: Creating an Early Care and Education System for America's Children*. Final Report. The Quality 2000 Initiative. New Haven, CT: The Bush Center in Child Development and Social Policy at Yale University, 1997. http://eric .ed.gov/?id=ED417027.

Kahane, Adam. *Power and Love: A Theory and Practice of Social Change*. San Francisco: Berrett-Koehler, 2010.

———. *Transformative Scenario Planning: Working Together to Change the Future*. San Francisco: Berrett-Koehler, 2012.

Kansas Leadership Center. *Civic Leadership Play Book*. Accessed March 16. Wichita, KS: Kansas Leadership Center, 2015. http://kansasleadershipcenter.org/sites/default/files/resources /klc_playbook.pdf.

Kegan, Robert, and Lisa Laskow Lahey. *How the Way We Talk Can Change the Way We Work: Seven Languages for Transformation*. San Francisco: Jossey-Bass, 2001.

———. *Immunity to Change: How to Overcome It and Unlock Potential in Yourself and Your Organization*. Boston: Harvard Business Press, 2009.

Kurtzman, Joel. *Common Purpose: How Great Leaders Get Organizations to Achieve the Extraordinary*. San Francisco: Jossey-Bass, 2010.

Linsky, Marty, and Ronald Heifetz. Foreword in *Ready or Not: Leadership Choices in Early Care and Education*, by Stacie. G. Goffin and Valora Washington, ix–xi. New York: Teachers College Press, 2007.

Meadows, Donella H. *Thinking in Systems: A Primer*. Edited by Diana Wright. White River Junction, VT: Chelsea Green, 2008.

National Association for the Education of Young Children. *Strategic Direction*. Washington, DC: National Association for the Education of Young Children, 2014. http://www .naeyc.org/files/naeyc/NAEYC_Strategic_Direction_2014.pdf.

National Council of Architectural Registration Boards. *The History of NCARB*. Washington, DC: National Council of Architectural Registration Boards, 2004. http://www.ncarb .org/~/media/files/pdf/special-paper/history.pdf.

Ready, Douglas A., and Emily Truelove. "The Power of Collective Ambition." *Harvard Business Review* 89, no. 2 (December 2011): 94–102.

Roberts, Charlotte. "What You Can Expect . . . in Working with Mental Models." In *The Fifth Discipline Fieldbook: Strategies and Tools for Building a Learning Organization*, edited by Peter M. Senge, Art Kleiner, Charlotte Roberts, Richard B. Ross, and Bryan J. Smith, 239–42. New York: Currency, 1994.

Ross, Rick. "Skillful Discussion: Protocols for Reaching a Decision—Mindfully." In *The Fifth Discipline Fieldbook: Strategies and Tools for Building a Learning Organization*, edited by Peter M. Senge, Art Kleiner, Charlotte Roberts, Richard B. Ross, and Bryan J. Smith, 385–91. New York: Currency, 1994.

Ross, Rick, and Charlotte Roberts. "Balancing Inquiry and Advocacy." In *The Fifth Discipline Fieldbook: Strategies and Tools for Building a Learning Organization*, edited by Peter M. Senge, Art Kleiner, Charlotte Roberts, Richard B. Ross, and Bryan J. Smith, 254–9. New York: Currency, 1994.

Schumann, Mary Jean. Foreword in *Early Childhood Education for a New Era: Leading for Our Profession* by Stacie G. Goffin, xi–xiv. New York: Teachers College Press, 2013.

Senge, Peter M. *The Fifth Discipline: The Art and Practice of the Learning Organization*. New York: Doubleday, 1990.

———. Afterword in *The World Café: Shaping Our Futures through Conversations That Matter*, edited by Juanita Brown, 217–20. San Francisco: Berrett-Koehler, 2005.

Senge, Peter, Hal Hamilton, and John Kania. "The Dawn of System Leadership." *Stanford Social Innovation Review* 13, no. 1 (Winter 2015): 26–33.

Senge, Peter M., Art Kleiner, Charlotte Roberts, Richard B. Ross, and Bryan J. Smith, eds. *The Fifth Discipline Fieldbook: Strategies and Tools for Building a Learning Organization*. New York: Currency, 1994.

Senge, Peter, C. Otto Scharmer, Joseph Jaworski, and Betty Sue Flowers. *Presence: An Exploration of Profound Change in People, Organizations, and Society*. New York: Currency, 2005.

Senge, Peter, Bryan Smith, Nina Kruschwitz, Joe Laur, and Sara Schley. *The Necessary Revolution: How Individuals and Organizations Are Working Together to Create a Sustainable World*. New York: Broadway Books, 2010.

Shonkoff, Jack P. "Protecting Brains, Not Simply Stimulating Minds." *Science* 333, no. 6045 (August 2011): 982–3.

Spodek, Bernard, and Herbert J. Walberg, eds. Introduction in *Early Childhood Education: Issues and Insights*, 1–7. Berkeley, CA: McCutchan Publishing, 1977.

Stanfield, Brian. *The Art of Focused Conversation: 100 Ways to Access Group Wisdom in the Workplace*. Gabriola Island, Canada: New Society Publishers, 2000.

Starr, Paul. *The Social Transformation of American Medicine: The Rise of a Sovereign Profession and the Making of a Vast Industry*. New York: Basic Books, 1984.

Stone, Douglas, Bruce Patton, and Sheila Heen. *Difficult Conversations: How to Discuss What Matters Most*. New York: Penguin Books, 1999.

Vogt, Eric E., Juanita Brown, and David Isaacs. *The Art of Powerful Questions: Catalyzing Insight, Innovation, and Action*. Mills Valley, CA: Whole Systems Associates, 2003. https://www.principals.ca/Documents/powerful_questions_article_(World_Cafe_Website).pdf

Wheatley, Margaret J. *Leadership and the New Science: Discovering Order in a Chaotic World*. San Francisco: Berrett-Koehler, 1992.

White, Sheldon H., and Steve L. Buka. "Early Education: Programs, Traditions, and Policies." *Review of Research in Education* 14, no. 1 (January 1987): 43–97.

Woods, Mary N. *From Craft to Profession: The Practice of Architecture in Nineteenth-Century America*. Berkeley: University of California Press, 1999.

Zander, Rosamund Stone, and Benjamin Zander. *The Art of Possibility: Transforming Professional and Personal Life*. Boston: Harvard Business School Press, 2000.

DATE DUE

About the Author

recognized authority and author in early childhood edu-
raising the competence of ECE as a field of practice. She
d development from the University of Massachusetts—
r master's in early childhood—special education from
iversity, an advanced certificate in education from Johns
her doctorate from the University of Houston. Stacie
rincipal of the Goffin Strategies Group, where she uses
s to improve the effectiveness of programs and services
gh leadership, capacity, and systems development. She is
ood *Education for a New Era: Leading for Our Profession.*